Your Language · *One*

This is the first of a series of three books

Topics dealt with in this book include:

- Skills of group discussion
- Non-verbal communication
- The development of writing systems
- The difference between the spoken
  and written word
- The structure of the sentences
- The use and function of the dictionary
- Slangs and the language of
  different communities
- The development of English
- The influence of other languages
  on English
- The forms and functions of local
  dialects and standard English
- Using context clues in reading
- Different reading strategies
- Using an index
- Proof reading
- Use of paragraphs in reading
  and writing
- Planning writing

Your Language · *One*

MAURA HEALY

Deputy Head, Quintin Kynaston School,
North London

M

Macmillan Education

For John and Geoffrey

First published 1981

Published by
MACMILLAN EDUCATION LIMITED
Houndmills Basingstoke Hampshire RG21 2XS
and London
Associated companies in Delhi Dublin
Hong Kong Johannesburg Lagos Melbourne
New York Singapore and Tokyo

Printed in Hong Kong

British Library Cataloguing in Publication Data

Healy, Maura
Your language one.
1. English language – Composition and exercises
I. Title
428   PE1408

ISBN 0-333-28167-5

Contents

Acknowledgements

The author and publishers wish to acknowledge the following photograph sources:

BBC Hulton Picture Library p. 84; Camera Press – Fenilla C Dening p. 89; J Allan Cash Limited p. 54; Ron Chapman p. 55; Colorphoto Hans Hinz SWB p. 25; Henry Grant pp. 16, 17, 91; Richard and Sally Greenhill pp. 67, 76; Dr Hans Hass pp. 20, 21; John Hillelson Agency Limited – Ian Berry p. 19; The Louvre, Paris p. 22; Rank Film Distributors p. 18 top; John Topham Picture Library pp. 18 bottom, 33; Taken from the Publication *Looking at Nigeria* by Colin Latcham published by Adam and Charles Black p. 74; The Willow Restaurant – photographer Jim Brownbill p. 83.

The author and publishers wish to thank the following who have kindly given permission for the use of copyright material:

Adam & Charles Black (Publishers) Ltd. for the index page from *Looking at China* by Noel Gray; William Blackwood & Sons Ltd. for 'Buzzing Death' from *Tea Pests* by J. Beagle-Atkins; Camera Press Ltd. for an article from the *Observer Magazine* July 30, 1978; Rex Collings Ltd. for an extract from *Watership Down* by Richard Adams; Evans Bros. Ltd. for 'The Discovery of the New World' and 'The Thirteen Colonies' from *A Visual History of the United States* by Hall & Case; Faber & Faber Ltd. and Doubleday & Co. Inc. for an excerpt from 'Old Florist' © 1946 by Harper & Brothers from *The Collected Poems of Theodore Roethke*; Hamish Hamilton Ltd. and Harper & Row Publishers Inc. for extracts from 'Louis Goes to School' in *The Trumpet of the Swan* by E. B. White; George G. Harrap & Co. Ltd. for extracts from *Goalkeeper's Revenge and Other Stories* by Bill Naughton; Irene Josephy on behalf of Geoffrey Willans and Ronald Searle for extracts from *How to be Topp*; Oxford University Press Ltd. for extracts from *The Concise Oxford Dictionary* (6th edn 1976) and *The Oxford Paperback Dictionary* (1979); Penguin Books Ltd. for an extract from *The Drummer Boy* by Leon Garfield; Laurence Pollinger Ltd. on behalf of Grace Zia Chu for an extract and recipe from *The Pleasures of Chinese Cooking* published by Faber & Faber Ltd; The Schools Council for extracts from *The Quality of Listening* by A. Wilkinson *et al.* (Schools Council Research Studies, Macmillan Education 1974); Mrs A. M. Walsh for the poem 'The New Boy' from *The Truants* by John Walsh; Ward Lock Educational Ltd. for extracts from *Classroom Encounters* ed. Mike Torbe and Robert Protherough, and with the Schools Council for an extract from *Language Policies in Schools*; A. P. Watt on behalf of the National Trust for an extract from 'How the Alphabet Was Made' from *Just So Stories* by Rudyard Kipling; English Centre, Ebury Teachers' Centre, for extracts from *Jamaica Child* by Errol O'Connor, and *Small Accidents* by Sabir Bandali.

The publishers have made every effort to trace the copyright holders, but if they have inadvertently overlooked any, they will be pleased to make the necessary arrangements at the earliest opportunity.

Teaching points

1   Talking together   *p. 11*
Time: Two lessons
Equipment: None
Aim: To introduce and explain the
   function of group discussion
Activity: An analysis of a transcript of
   three eleven-year-old pupils
   discussing a poem
   Group discussion
Follow-up: Unit 2 'Working in
   groups' 6 'The difference between
   writing and talking'

2   Working in groups   *p. 15*
Time: Two lessons
Equipment: Tape recorders, preferably
   one per group, would be helpful,
   but are not essential
Aim: To explain value of group work
   and set guidelines
Activity: Group discussion of a poem
Further activities: Writing based on
   poem

3   Making contact   *p. 17*
Time: Two lessons
Equipment: None
Aim: To show how we communicate
   without words
Activity: Group discussion.
   Drawing cartoon strips
Follow-up: Unit 4 'Writing and
   talking'
   5 'Choosing between writing and
   talking'
   6 'The difference between writing
   and talking'
Further activities: Mime
   Watching television with the sound
   off
   Writing descriptions of appearance
   of people/animals in different
   moods
   Using more cartoon strips of
   different types ('Superman', love
   stories etc.) and discussing why so
   few words are needed.

4   Writing and talking   *p. 24*
Time: Two lessons
Equipment: None
Aim: To encourage pupils to consider
   why and how different writing
   systems developed
   Discussion of the development of
   ideographs and different alphabets
Pupil activity: Picture writing
   Making up story as to how three
   or four letters of our alphabet
   came to be made
Follow-up: Unit 5 'Choosing between
   writing and talking'
   6 'The difference between writing
   and talking'

**5   Choosing between writing
and talking**   *p. 29*
Time: Two lessons
Equipment: None
Aim: To encourage pupils to consider
   why we write in some situations
   and talk in others
Activity: Group discussion
   Writing short play or story
Follow-up: Unit 6 'The difference
   between writing and talking'

**6   The difference between
writing and talking**   *p. 33*
Time: Two lessons
Equipment: At least one tape
   recorder, preferably one per group
Aim: To begin to identify some of
   the differences between writing and
   talking e.g. grammatical structure,
   use of fillers and repetition
Activity: Discussion of transcript and
   essay on same topic
   Making and recording prepared
   talks on favourite books
   Recording ensuing discussion
   Comparing discussion with formal
   talk
Follow-up: Unit 7 'Using sentences in
   writing'
   (The talks on books are used again
   in unit 7.)

7   Using sentences in writing   *p. 35*
Time: Two lessons and time for
   interviewing and further two
   lessons for writing up interviews
   and preparing display

Equipment: At least one tape recorder
   needed for second half of unit
Aim: To increase understanding of
   the conventions of writing,
   particularly the use of the sentence
Activity: Group discussion of
   transcripts
   Rewriting of transcript
   Questionnaire design
   Interviewing
   Writing up interviews
   Preparing display
Follow-up: Unit 8 'Making sentences'
   9 'Finding patterns in sentences 1'
   10 'Finding patterns in sentences
   2'

8   Making sentences   *p. 38*
Time: One lesson
Equipment: None
Aim: To explore possibilities of
   sentence structure by contracting
   and expanding sentences
Activity: Groups devise two very long
   sentences and contract one
Follow-up: Unit 9 'Finding patterns
   in sentences 1'
   10 'Finding patterns in sentences
   2'

**9   Finding patterns in
sentences 1**   *p. 39*
Time: One lesson
Equipment: None
Aim: To show presence of patterns in
   sentences, introduce concept of
   noun and adjective
Activity: Pupils produce own nonsense
   sentences and ask each other
   'multiple choice' questions about
   them
   Identify own 'nonsense' nouns and
   adjectives
Follow-up: Unit 10 'Finding patterns
   in sentences 2'

**10   Finding patterns in
sentences 2**   *p. 40*
Time: Two lessons
Equipment: None
Aim: To introduce verbs
   Give context for writing for
   specified audience
Activities: Identifying verbs in pupils'
   own nonsense sentences

Cloze passage
Continuing cloze story
Proof-reading and editing
continuation of story for other
classes to use as cloze passage
Follow-up: Unit 25 'Proof-reading
your work' may be useful here

11 Using a dictionary 1 *p. 42*

Time: One lesson
Equipment: A dictionary for each
pupil
Aim: To explain the function of the
dictionary and introduce concept
of guide words, alphabetical order
and some strategies for guessing
initial letters in a word
Activities: Group or individual work
on using guide words
Putting words in alphabetical order
Making intelligent guesses at initial
letters
Follow-up: Unit 12 'Using a
dictionary 2'
13 'Making your own dictionary'

12 Using a dictionary 2 *p. 45*

Time: Two lessons
Equipment: A dictionary for each
pupil
Aim: To demonstrate how
dictionaries offer guides to
pronunciation and usage
Concept of syllable, stress, and
adverb introduced
Activity: Group discussion of
examples
Comparison with other dictionaries
List of slang words not found in
dictionary
Follow-up: Unit 13 Making your own
dictionary

13 Making your own
dictionary *p. 47*

Time: Two lessons and time for
interviewing
Equipment: A dictionary of slang
would be helpful
Note books for individual
dictionaries
Aim: (1) To explain the layout,
symbols, and conventions of a
dictionary
(2) To stimulate discussion about

slang and how our language
changes
Activity: Group discussion
Interviewing older people
Compilation of class or group
dictionary of slang
Beginning to make individual,
personal dictionary
Follow-up: Unit 14 'How English
grew'
15 'Is there only one English?'
16 'Our changing language'
17 'Using standard English'
18 'What about proper English?'
19 'The language of school'

14 How English grew *p. 49*

Time: Two lessons
Equipment: One or more dictionaries
which show word origin, for
example *Concise Oxford*
Aim: To show the diversity of the
English language
To recognise the range of
languages which may be spoken in
one class
To demonstrate the use of the
etymological reference
Activity: Looking up etymological
references
Making checklist of languages
spoken in class
Adding a section to the class or
group dictionary – 'Words English
has borrowed from languages
spoken in our class'
Follow-up: Unit 15 'Is there only one
English?'
16 'Our changing language'
17 'Using standard English'
18 'What about proper English?'
19 'The language of school'

15 Is there only one English? *p. 51*

Time: Two lessons
Equipment: Tape recorder
Aim: To show a range of dialects
including standard English
Activity: Changing non-standard
dialect into standard and noting
change in spelling, vocabulary and
accents
Making tapes of dialects used in
class and discussing them
Follow-up: Unit 16 'Our changing

language'
17 'Using standard English'
18 'What about proper English?'
19 'The language of school'

16 Our changing language *p. 53*

Time: Two lessons
Equipment: An American/English
dictionary would be useful
Aim: To develop an understanding of
how language changes and
develops
Activity: Translation of Caxton
Looking at playground language
American language
Rhyming slang
Dialects used in class
Adding sections to class/group
dictionary
Follow-up: Unit 17 'Using standard
English'
18 'What about proper English?'
19 'The language of school'

17 Using standard English *p. 57*

Time: Two lessons
Equipment: A tape recorder would be
useful for the second half of the
unit
Aim: To consider the contexts in
which standard English is
appropriate
Activity: Group discussion
Writing and recording a story or
play
Follow-up: Unit 18 'What about
proper English?'

18 What about proper English? *p. 55*

Time: Two lessons
Equipment: None
Aim: To put the notion of 'proper
English' in perspective
Activity: Group discussion
Individual writing
(1) about dialect
(2) a story or play
Follow-up: Unit 19 'The language of
school'

19 The language of school *p. 60*

Time: Three lessons
Equipment: None
Aim: To show how organisations
develop their own particular

languages
To show the organisational pattern of the school
To encourage realistic self-assessment

Activity: Listing specialist school words
Adding this section to class/group dictionary
Writing own reports
Survey
Drawing up a 'who's who' of the school

Follow-up: The specialist words and 'who's who' are used again in unit 28 'Using paragraphs to plan writing'

20   Words need words   *p. 62*

Time: One lesson

Equipment: None

Aim: To show how context gives clues as to meaning of unfamiliar words

Activity: Group discussion of meanings of words in the poem 'Jabberwocky'
Comparing group's interpretation with that of 'Humpty Dumpty'

Follow-up: Unit 21 'Using context clues'

21   Using context clues   *p. 65*

Time: Two lessons

Equipment: None

Aim: To identify particular types of clues

Activity: Group discussion, making intelligent guesses at meaning
Identifying types of clues
Using context clues to illuminate nonsense or difficult words

Follow-up: Unit 22 'How do we read?'

22   How do we read?   *p. 67*

Time: Three lessons

Equipment: None

Aim: To demonstrate how reading involves guessing

Activity: Analysis of transcript
Quick reading of cloze passage
Detailed cloze
Preparing another cloze passage for another class to use
Writing for specified audience

Follow-up: Unit 23 'Reading in different ways'
25 'Proof-reading your work' is useful here

23   Reading in different ways   *p. 72*

Time: Two lessons

Equipment: None

Aim: To demonstrate the techniques and uses of skimming and scanning

Activity: Skimming one passage and scanning a map and a passage

Follow-up: Unit 24 'Using an index'
26 'Paragraphs are sense units'
Useful work may also be done using a variety of school textbooks

24   Using an index   *p. 76*

Time: One lesson

Equipment: None

Aim: To demonstrate the conventions of a simple index

Activity: Finding page references
Discussing in groups the variety of ways items may be indexed

Follow-up: Indexes in school textbooks or other non-fiction material could be usefully studied

25   Proof-reading your work   *p. 78*

Time: Two lessons

Equipment: None

Aim: To show uses and techniques of proof-reading

Activity: Proof-reading an extract from *How to be Topp*
Learning proof-reading signs

Follow-up: Proof-reading skills to be used in all written work

26   Paragraphs are sense units   *p. 82*

Time: Three lessons

Equipment: None

Aim: To show the functions of paragraphs

Activity: Group discussion of examples
Sequencing a recipe
Designing a game and its rules
Sequencing instructions

Follow-up: Unit 27 'Looking at paragraphs'
28 'Using paragraphs to plan writing'
29 'Using diagrams to plan writing'

27   Looking at paragraphs   *p. 87*

Time: Two lessons

Equipment: None

Aim: To show that paragraphs all have particular topics
Identify introductory and concluding paragraphs

Activity: Identifying topics of a series of paragraphs
Paragraphing a short article

Follow-up: Unit 28 'Using paragraphs to plan writing'
29 'Using diagrams to plan writing'

28   Using paragraphs to plan writing   *p. 90*

Time: Four lessons

Equipment: None, but material collected earlier will be useful: school language dictionary, 'who's who' in the school ('The language of school'), languages and dialects spoken in the class ('How English grew' and 'Our changing language'), school rules game ('Paragraphs are sense units')
'Proof-reading your work' should be done before this unit is tackled

Aim: To show how paragraphs can be used to sequence and order a complex writing task
To bring together previous pupil research
To develop proof-reading and editing skills
Writing for a specified audience

Activity: Compiling, editing and proof-reading a pamphlet on the school for next year's first year

Follow-up: Unit 29 'Using diagrams to plan writing'

29   Using diagrams to plan writing   *p. 93*

Time: Two lessons

Equipment: None

Aim: To show how diagrams may be used instead of notes to organise a piece of writing
To encourage discussion as to how school library works

Activity: Planning addition to pamphlet – Our school library

9

Unit 1
Talking together

I expect you have found many differences between your primary school and your new secondary school. One of the things pupils often find difficult at first is working out when they are allowed to talk and when they should be silent.

You meet many more teachers in the course of a day now, and each one may well expect you to work in a slightly different way but in most of your lessons you will need, at some time or other, to work with a group of other people. How can you learn to do that well? Let's start by looking at a group of pupils discussing a poem together.

Look at this transcript, that is, a written version of a conversation or discussion. Three girls of your age have chosen to discuss a poem called 'Old Florist' by Theodore Roethke. Their teacher was not present. A transcript was later made from a tape of their discussion.

Occasionally the transcript says 'indecipherable' – that means that the person making the transcript could not understand what was being said. The girls' initials come before their words so you can tell who's speaking. Occasionally there is a ? instead of an initial. Why do you think that is?

When you read the transcript, it may seem strange. This is because it gives exactly what everyone says, including 'mm' and 'er'. Normally the things you read have none of these features because the way we write is quite different from the way we speak. We will look at this difference in more detail later, in the unit called 'The difference between talking and writing'.

● Divide yourselves into groups of between three and six in order to read the transcript out loud. There are two reasons for this:

1 You will be able to follow the transcript much better if you read it aloud like a play. There are three pupils involved in the transcript so three of you will need to read the 'parts'.

2 There are several questions at the end of each section for you to discuss with a group of friends.

When you have read and discussed each section you should read the whole transcript through again so you can see how the discussion developed.

Who's going to read the first poem, Susan?
S: Yes . . . What. 'Old Florist'?
J: Yeah.
S: (coughs)

> *That hump of a man bunching*
>   *chrysanthemums*
> *or pinching back ast . . . asters*
> *or planting azaleas*
> *tramping and stamping dirt into pots*
> *how he could flick and pick rotten leaves*
> *or yellowy petals*
> *or scoop out a weed close to flourishing*
>   *roots*
> *or make the dust buzz with a light spray*
> *or drown a bug in one spit of tobacco juice*
> *or fan life into a wilted sweet pea with his*
>   *hat*
> *or stand all night watering roses*
> *his feet blue in rubber boots*

J: Well this rem . . . reminds me of a poem, well, when we had to write a poem on a stranger in class . . .
S: Oh yes.
J: I wrote one on a gardener. I'd never . . . he was at a hotel we'd stayed at but this reminds me of the sort of person that I thought *he* was, the person who's got nothing to do *except* for his flowers, so he does everything for his flowers and for nothing else, no wife or anything, but for his flowers.
S: Yes, he works in one of those big um gardens that are owned by people.
(Yes, from someone)
Perhaps, perhaps, perhaps by this poem, not by this poem but from my thoughts, perhaps he, perhaps he didn't like the people who own, who owned, the garden at all, he just likes the garden but not the people, he's

devoted (continues but indecipherable with interruption).
J: Oh I think he's probably um likes the people but he's he doesn't spend any time with them he just says good morning and goodnight like people usually do but he spends a lot ah . . . nearly all his time in the garden making it trying to make it look better and better as the days go by (three voices together).

● Things to discuss:
1 Did you notice how J compared the gardener in the poem to one whom she had seen at a hotel? She had written a poem about that other gardener. Do you think that she was able to understand this poem better because she had already written one on a similar topic? Discuss how that might have helped.

2 How does J help the group to see how she imagines the gardener in the poem?

3 S already has a theory about the gardener. She thinks she can begin to understand him. What idea has she had about him?

The transcript continues. L, who hasn't spoken yet, is thinking about what the others have said. She says 'Mmm'. Have you noticed we often use words like 'Mmm' or 'Oh' or 'Yes' to reassure people who are talking to us that we are thinking about what they are saying? It's a way of saying, 'Don't worry I'm with you'. Listen to someone listening on the phone and you'll hear lots of 'Mmms'.

L: Mmm.
S: I think that's what he *does*.
L: He might have had a sort of upset in the very upset him he's devoted himself completely to flowers and plants and that and all he cares about is how his beautiful flowers grow and if one dies he'll try and bring it back to life again and make it live (two voices together).
?: Like it says poems . . .

●
1 L has been listening to what J and S have said. She has taken their ideas and added her own. What reason does she give to explain why the gardener is so interested in his flowers?

2 How does her idea add to the points J and S have made?

●
1 What has happened in the discussion to make her change her mind?

2 How has being able to *talk* it through helped her to *think* it through?

Now read on.

S: I don't like the line where it says 'Or drown a bug in one spit of tobacco juice' it's put nicely and um . . .

?: I like . . .
I don't like . . .

S: I know it could sound nice to someone but I don't . . .

L: It's just not nice for the flowers it's not . . .

S: . . . well, I suppose it . . . I suppose it looks it it it goes well with the poem . . . I was just thinking I don't I wouldn't drown a bug.

J: No but I think that with the nice verses about . . . nice lines about all the nice flowers and chrysanthemums and what else have you and but then the spit of tobacco juice it just it spoils the flowers (someone says 'Oh') it's out of place.

S: I say I don't think that, I think if you didn't have that in then it would be all one thing all one thing and um . . . like you haven't got it *all* about flowers you've got . . .

J: No.

S: Well it is something to do with flowers but that is as well because they they go on flowers don't they?

J: Yes I suppose it it does fit in yes it does now I come to think (long pause).

They are a bit worried about the line; 'Or drown a bug in one spit of tobacco juice' aren't they? J ends up saying:
'Yes, I suppose it does fit in, yes it does now I come to think,' although she had said that the line spoilt the poem about the 'nice flowers'.

Here is the last section.

S: Er I don't I don't see how he can stamp dirt in pots. I thought you just put it in (pause).
L: You do.
J: Oh yes . . . P'raps.
S: You stamp, oh you flatten it down though, don't you?
L: Yes.
S: I like that line, I can just see the picture of that line.
L: Yes.
S: That hump of a man bunching chrysanthemums.
L: Yes.
S: You can just see him with a great bunch of chrysanthemums growing in the garden and his sort of hump-shaped back bending over them trying to make them look nicer.
J: Mmm.
L: And when it says . . . how he could flick and pick rotten leaves or yellowy petals I can see him in the greenhouse with a . . . begonia pulling off the dead leaves and ones that are going yellow (mmm).
J: I think when it says um oh where is it? the line, oh yeah, 'Or scoop out a weed close to flourishing roots' er I think that shows how how long he's been a gardener because he can do it so well.
S: Yes.
J: It does, he's done, he's *known* it all his life.
S: That's the same as 'flick and pick'.
J: Yes, yes.
S: With me I'd just go up to it and look around quickly I wouldn't be able to flick it out though in case I broke the plant I'd have to take it out carefully.
J: But he's he *knows* all about it. Mmm.
L: Yes and it says 'or fan life into wilted sweet peas with his hat' er.
S: That's a good line.
L: Yes, yes.

S: That shows again the same sort of thing how he can do it. Like you you if you had a wilted pea you'd just give it up wouldn't you.
J: Yes but . . .
S: But he can do something with it.

● Can you see how they are sharing the excitement and enjoyment of the poem?

1 How are they helping each other to enjoy it?

2 What differences between themselves and the gardener do they discuss? Do you think they've understood him?

● Now you have looked closely at the transcript, when you have read it through again, you can discuss some general points.

1 Do you think the girls would have got most out of the poem if:
(a) They had read it by themselves and not discussed it?
(b) They had had it explained by their teacher?
(c) The teacher had discussed it with the whole class?
(d) They had read it together and discussed it as we have just seen.

2 Have you ever got into an argument during a group discussion? Can you think of ways in which you could avoid rows?

3 Have you ever found it valuable to explain something to a friend? If so, why was it so useful for you?

Unit 2
Working in groups

In the last unit we saw a group of pupils helping each other to enjoy a poem. They were very good at working together. They were not only learning about the poem, they were learning how to learn from others. Being able to work and discuss in groups is valuable because:

1 Being able to listen to what other people have to say and to be able to state your own point of view means that you can learn from others and sort out your own ideas. We all find that we do not know what we are going to say until we have said it. The act of actually saying something seems to help us clarify our thoughts. Do you remember how J sorted out her ideas about the line in the poem that was troubling her?

2 Very often when you are grappling with a new idea, however well a teacher or a text-book has explained it, you need to think it through and re-explain it in your own words in order to be able to understand it. It is often very useful to be asked to explain something to your friends because to do that you have to work out why it may be causing difficulty and find ways of making the problem simpler.

3 It is very useful to listen to other people talking through a new idea. In listening to them talking you are always checking with yourself, 'Do I agree?', or, 'Surely she's got it wrong'. Other people can show you ways of looking at things you had not thought of for yourself.

4 Listening and talking skills are not only valuable within school. You can gain a great deal from discussions with your friends and adults. Once you leave school and go to work you will have to listen and talk to other people in order to do your job.

Your parents and teachers might well complain that you talk too much! If you note carefully the times when you are told off for talking you will probably find that they are when:

1 What you are saying is irrelevant – it has nothing to do with the matter in hand.

2 You are not letting other people get a word in edgeways.

3 You are repetitious – saying the same thing over and over again.

Some guidelines for group discussion
1 Be prepared to *listen* and to change your mind.

2 Be polite – don't butt in when someone is in the middle of explaining something.

3 If you do disagree, do not just say 'Rubbish!' Disagree politely and explain why you think someone has got the wrong end of the stick.

4 Try to stick to the subject. In the transcript you looked at, it seemed for a moment as if J was going to wander off the topic, but it soon became clear that she had something useful to say.

Some ideas that might help
Choose a *chairperson* – make sure it is not the same person every time. His or her job is:
(a) to keep the discussion on the topic
(b) to ensure that everyone has a chance to speak.
  Choose a *secretary* – you should take turns at this job too. His or her job is to take brief notes of what you have said so that:
(a) you can report back to the whole class or to your teacher
(b) you can check what you have covered so far and see where your discussion might go from there.

It is very useful to *report back* to the whole class from time to time so that you can remind yourself what your group said, and, at the same time, see how other groups felt about similar topics.

● Now you try it. Here is a poem about a boy starting at a new school. Discuss it in groups. Before you start, choose your chairperson and your secretary. It would help a great deal if you could tape your discussion. Then you can play it back to your group or to the whole class and discuss how well your discussion worked. When you listen to the tape try to note down ideas about how the discussion could be improved next time.

Here is the poem. You will all have a lot to say about it, I expect, because you too have had that experience of coming to a strange, new school.

The New Boy

The door swung inward. I stood and breathed
The new-school atmosphere:
The smell of polish and disinfectant,
And the flavour of my own fear.

I followed into the cloakroom; the walls
Rang to the shattering noise
Of boys who barged and boys who banged;
Boys and still more boys!

A boot flew by me. Its angry owner
Pursued with force and yell;
Somewhere a man snapped orders; somewhere
There clanged a warning bell.

And there I hung with my new schoolmates;
They pushing and shoving me; I
Unknown, unwanted, pinned to the wall;
On the verge of ready-to-cry.

Then, from the doorway, a boy called out:
'Hey, you over there! You're new!
Don't just stand there propping the wall up!
I'll look after you!'

I turned; I timidly raised my eyes;
He stood and grinned meanwhile;
And my fear died, and my lips answered
Smile for his smile.

He showed me the basins, the rows of pegs;
He hung my cap at the end;
He led me away to my new classroom . . .
And now that boy's my friend.

John Walsh

Unit 3
Making contact

Have you noticed that people communicate or make contact with each other by using their bodies as well as by speaking and writing?

This girl is communicating her feelings very directly, isn't she? Words, either spoken or written, are unnecessary.

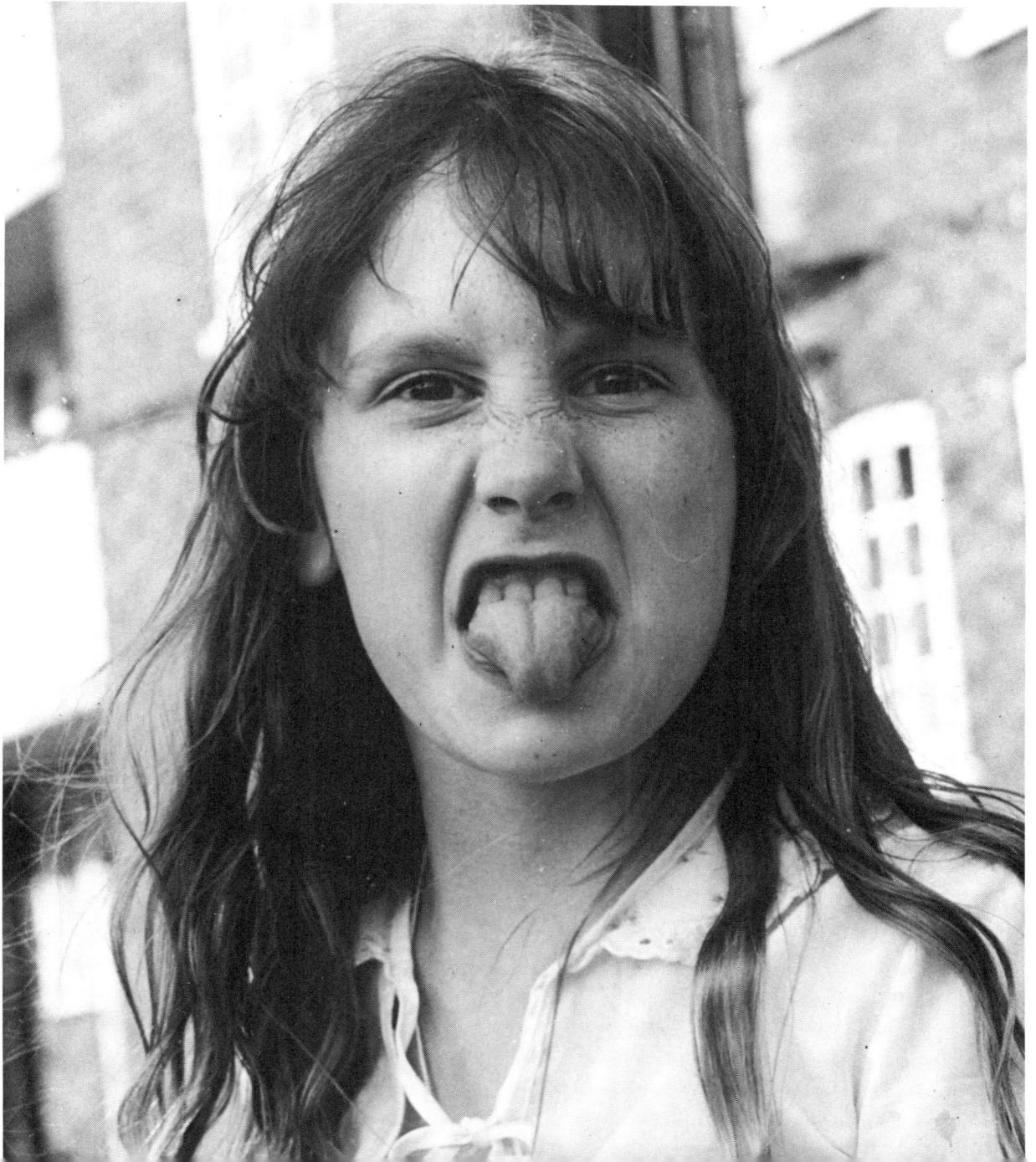

Here is another photograph. This time it comes from a film. Can you tell what the man is thinking? The expression on his face, the clenched fist, and the tense way he is standing give you all the information you need. Discuss this in your groups.

The actor, Richard Harris, is in fact giving out the same signal as this bearded lizard. Its gaping mouth suggests its anger. The inside of the mouth is brilliantly coloured. This makes the animal seem even more fearsome.

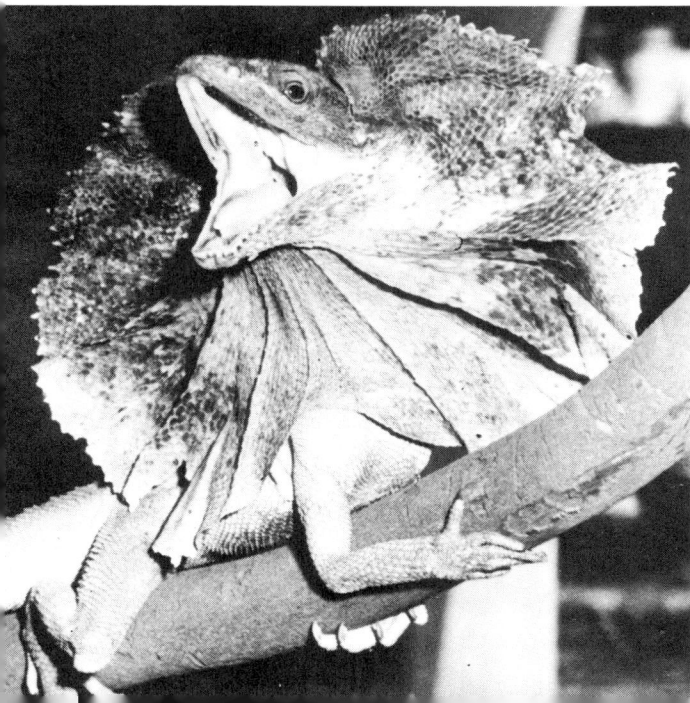

Have you noticed your pets giving out similar signs? What does a dog do as well as growl or bark when he is angry? What does a cat do as well as hiss and spit to show he is cross?

● Draw a picture of an angry cat and discuss with your group the ways the animal communicates with its body. We could call this body language.

We don't use body language only to show anger. Look at this diagram. It shows male fiddler crabs going through a series of movements which involve waving the larger of their two claws. They are signalling to attract female fiddler crabs.

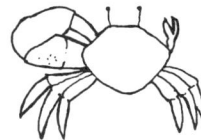

1

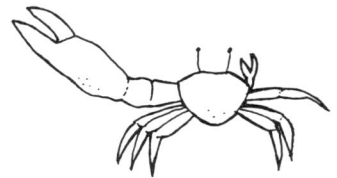

4

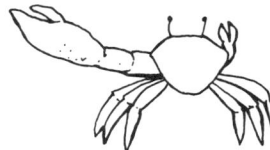

2

5

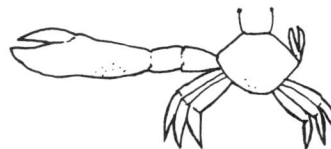

3

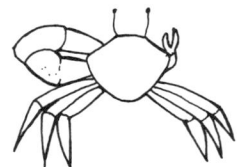

6

Here are two boys dancing. They are doing exactly the same thing. They are using their bodies to attract females!

We use our faces as well as the rest of our bodies to communicate with others. Look at this series of pictures. Discuss in your groups what emotions you think the woman is feeling. She did not know the photographs were being taken and so her expression is quite natural.

The real story is that she has lost her child in a crowd. She looks helpless and sad. Try to write down the thoughts that are going through her mind.

Now here is a series of photographs of a
Japanese actress. She is acting a scene in which
she has just received bad news. In your groups
discuss the ways her face communicates her
feelings.

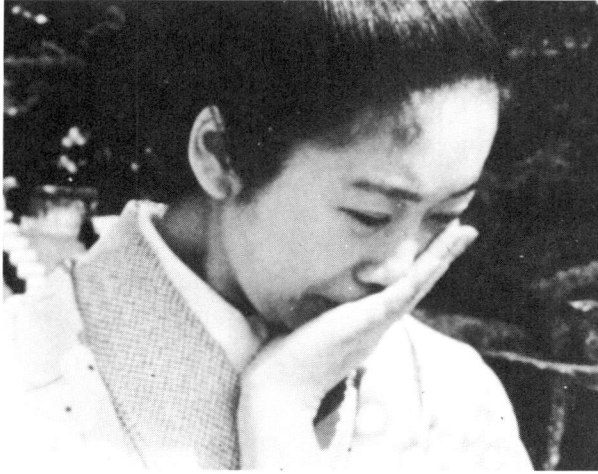

Finally, here is one of the world's most famous paintings, The Mona Lisa by Leonardo da Vinci. For centuries people have been puzzled by her smile. Is it happy or sad? In your groups again try to write down the thoughts that might be going through her mind.

● In your groups discuss ways in which we communicate using our bodies rather than words. You could discuss some of the following questions.

1 How is it that you can tell sometimes that your teacher is in a bad mood before he or she even speaks?

2 Sometimes fights nearly break out in school or in your neighbourhood. How do the people in the fights first of all show how angry they are, and then back down again? Remember you are not discussing the words they speak, but the ways in which their bodies show their feelings.

3 Have you ever watched animals in the zoo? How do they communicate with each other? Think of the chimpanzees, have you watched their behaviour?

4 Try acting out a variety of situations: getting good news, being sent to the head teacher because you've been rude, trying to get extra pocket money from your parents, going to a disco. Use words as well as actions to act out your scenes, but discuss in your groups how you use body language as well as words.

When you're watching television at home or watching a video-recording at school, ask if you can turn the sound right down. How much can you learn about what is going on without hearing the words?

● Look at the cartoon strip opposite. The 'balloons' which would normally contain the words the characters speak are empty. Can you guess what they are saying?

● Can you make a story from this or begin another story in a cartoon strip? Plan and draw it in your groups, leaving out the words as in the cartoon here. Then pass your cartoon to another group and ask them to fill in the words. Discuss the result!

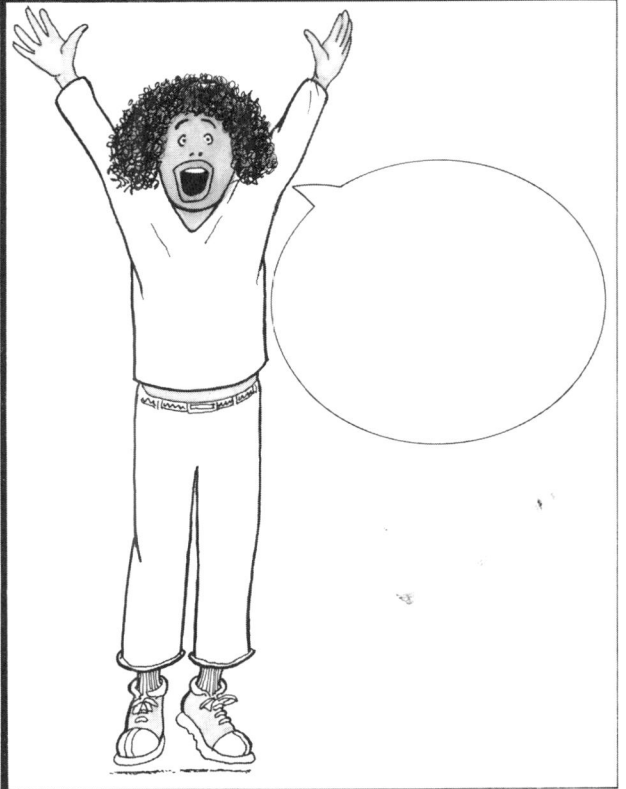

Unit 4
Writing and talking

When we write to someone or speak to them we are communicating, but we are communicating in very different ways. Look back at the tape transcript of the girls discussing the poem in 'Talking together' and you will see that people speak in a very different way from the way they write. We look at this in detail in the unit called 'The difference between writing and talking'.

Why do we need to write? We are so used to seeing the written word, we take it for granted. Just think what the world would be like without it.

We would not know our own history. The story of our past would be handed down by word of mouth and would change each time it was told.

There would have been no great scientific developments. Scientists have written down their theories and other scientists have been able to learn from them and go beyond them.

We would not know much about the rest of the world. Maps rely on words as well as pictures.

We would have to rely on the people around us for information.

We would only hear the stories that people we met were willing to tell us. We would not be able to read stories or novels for our own pleasure.

These are just a very few of the things we would miss if there was no writing. In your groups discuss what other things we would miss. How would you know what lesson to go to without a timetable? There are many things you can think of.

Make a list and share your ideas with other groups. Would you be able to remember them all if you had not written them down?

How did writing begin?

It is very odd, when you think of it, that these squiggles on a page make sense to you and to anyone else who can read English. How do we decide which squiggles mean what?

Some languages developed from pictures. Before people wrote words, they drew pictures to show others what they wanted. This is what you could do if you wanted something in a foreign country and did not know the words to ask for it. If you wanted an umbrella in Moscow, you could draw a picture of an umbrella and show it to the assistant.

American Indian picture writing works in the same way. The Indians could speak to each other in a way that you could not speak to the Russian shop assistant, but if they wanted to send a message or describe the history of the tribe they would draw pictures. Here are some examples of their pictures.

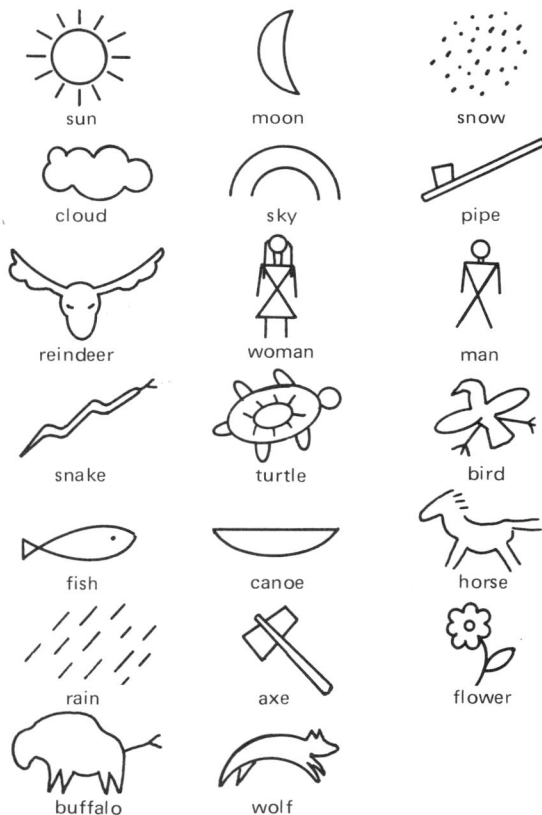

sun   moon   snow
cloud   sky   pipe
reindeer   woman   man
snake   turtle   bird
fish   canoe   horse
rain   axe   flower
buffalo   wolf

It is possible to make up a story by combining the pictures, because the pictures begin to be associated with an idea. We call them *ideographs* ('graph' means to write or draw and 'ideo' means symbolising or representing an idea). So the pipe came to mean peace and the axe, war. A picture of the sun meant a day and a picture of the moon meant a month. Can you make up a story with these pictures? Here is an example for you.

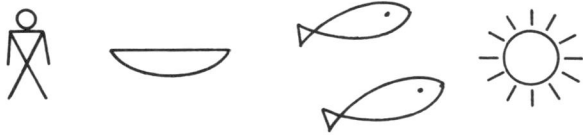

It means a man in a canoe caught two fishes in one day.

Here is another example of picture writing. This time it comes from England. It is a bill made out by a bricklayer who could not read or write. Can you guess what it means?

It reads: 'Two men and a boy, three-quarters of a day, two hods of mortar, ten shillings and sixpence'. The picture of the hanged man means 'account settled'.

● Now try to make up your own picture stories. You can use the American Indian symbols or invent your own. When you have made up your story see how many people in the class can understand it.

You have probably seen pictures of cave drawings before. These too tell stories, but some were made to work magic on the people or animals painted. Here is an example of a cave painting thousands of years old.

The Chinese writing system is based on ideographs. Each letter, or character, is really a tiny drawing, and the Chinese equivalent to our alphabet has over one thousand characters. Each character has developed from a simple picture into something more complicated. Here are some examples.

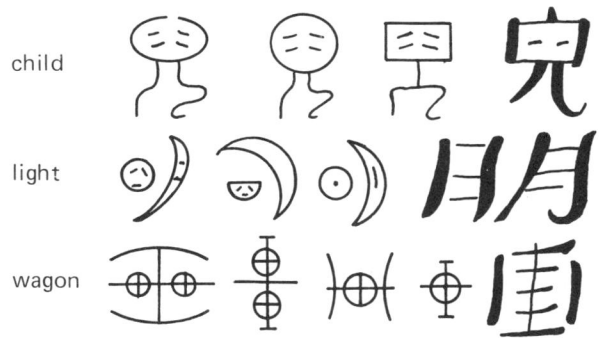

Other languages, like ours, developed their writing system in a very different way. Instead of drawing pictures of things, letters were devised to represent sounds. The Egyptians

25

were one of the earliest peoples to develop this system. The Egyptian word for water was 'Nu', and water was represented by a wavy line. Gradually the wavy line came to represent the sound of N. Their word for mouth was 'Ro', and the simplified drawing of a mouth came to represent the sound 'R', and so on, until they had developed twenty-five letter sounds. Many countries developed their own separate alphabets. There have been nearly two hundred different alphabets in different parts of the world and there are still about fifty in use apart from our own.

Here are some examples of different alphabets. These three sentences all say the same thing, 'My name is Pratiba'. The third sentence, written in Swahili, uses the same alphabet as we do in English, but the first two sentences use different alphabets. Not only are the letters different, but Pratiba writes the letters below the line _____

_____ like this.

GUJARATI   મારૂ નામ પ્રતિભા છે.

HINDI   मेरा नाम प्रतिभा है।

SWAHILI   _Jinna Yangu eko Pratibha._

Here Maria, a Greek girl, has written out a similar sentence, 'My name is Maria' using the Greek alphabet.

GREEK   Τὸ ὄνομα μου Εἶναι Μαρία

● There may be people in your class who can read and write in a language which has its own alphabet. You could mount a class display of their writing in those alphabets and discuss the differences between them and the alphabet English uses.

● Now here is an extract from one of Rudyard Kipling's *Just So Stories* in which he imagines what might have happened if a young girl called Taffimai Metallumai, Taffy for short, had tried to invent an alphabet. When you have read it make up your own story about how three or four of the letters of our alphabet came to be made.

How the Alphabet was Made

' But wasn't it inciting ! ' said Taffy. ' Don't you remember how the Head Chief puffed out his cheeks, and how funny the nice Stranger-man looked with the mud in his hair ? '

' Well do I,' said Tegumai. ' I had to pay two deerskins—soft ones with fringes—to the Stranger-man for the things we did to him.'

' *We* didn't do anything,' said Taffy. ' It was Mummy and the other Neolithic ladies—and the mud.'

' We won't talk about that,' said her Daddy. ' Let's have lunch.'

Taffy took a marrow-bone and sat mousy-quiet for ten whole minutes, while her Daddy scratched on pieces of birch-bark with a shark's tooth. Then she said, ' Daddy, I've thinked of a secret surprise. You make a noise—any sort of noise.'

' Ah ! ' said Tegumai. ' Will that do to begin with ? '

' Yes,' said Taffy. ' You look just like a carp-fish with its mouth open. Say it again, please.'

' Ah ! ah ! ah ! ' said her Daddy. ' Don't be rude, my daughter.'

' I'm not meaning rude, really and truly,' said Taffy. ' It's part of my secret-surprise-think. *Do* say *ah*, Daddy, and keep your mouth open at the end, and lend me that tooth. I'm going to draw a carp-fish's mouth wide-open.'

' What for ? ' said her Daddy.

' Don't you see ? ' said Taffy, scratching away on the bark. ' That will be our little secret s'prise. When I draw a carp-fish with his mouth open in the smoke at the back of our Cave—if Mummy doesn't mind—it will remind you of that ah-noise. Then we can play that it was me jumped out of the dark and s'prised you with that noise—same as I did in the beaver-swamp last winter.'

'Really?' said her Daddy, in the voice that grown-ups use when they are truly attending. 'Go on, Taffy.'

'Oh, bother!' she said. 'I can't draw all of a carp-fish, but I can draw something that means a carp-fish's mouth. Don't you know how they stand on their heads rooting in the mud? Well, here's a pretence carp-fish (we can play that the rest of him is drawn). Here's just his mouth, and that means *ah*.' And she drew this. (1.)

That's not bad,' said Tegumai, and scratched on his own piece of bark for himself; 'but you've forgotten the feeler that hangs across his mouth.'

'But I can't draw, Daddy.'

'You needn't draw anything of him except just the opening of his mouth and the feeler across. Then we'll know he's a carp-fish, 'cause the perches and trouts haven't got feelers. Look here, Taffy.' And he drew this. (2.)

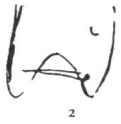

'Now I'll copy it,' said Taffy. 'Will you understand *this* when you see it?' And she drew this. (3.)

'Perfectly,' said her Daddy. 'And I'll be quite as s'prised when I see it anywhere, as if you had jumped out from behind a tree and said "Ah!"'

'Now, make another noise,' said Taffy, very proud.

'Yah!' said her Daddy, very loud.

'H'm,' said Taffy. 'That's a mixy noise. The end part is *ah*-carp-fish-mouth; but what can we do about the front part? *Yer-yer-yer* and *ah! Yah!*'

'It's very like the carp-fish-mouth noise. Let's draw another bit of the carp-fish and join 'em,' said her Daddy. *He* was quite incited too.

'No. If they're joined, I'll forget. Draw it separate. Draw his tail. If he's standing on his head the tail will come first. 'Sides, I think I can draw tails easiest,' said Taffy.

'A good notion,' said Tegumai. 'Here's a carp-fish tail for the *yer*-noise.' And he drew this. (4.)

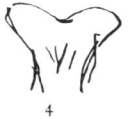

'I'll try now,' said Taffy. ''Member I can't draw like you, Daddy. Will it do if I just draw the split part of the tail, and a sticky-down line for where it joins?' And she drew this. (5.)

Her Daddy nodded, and his eyes were shiny bright with 'citement.

'That's beautiful,' she said. 'Now make another noise, Daddy.'

'Oh!' said her Daddy, very loud.

'That's quite easy,' said Taffy. 'You make your mouth all round like an egg or a stone. So an egg or a stone will do for that.'

'You can't always find eggs or stones. We'll have to scratch a round something like one.' And he drew this. (6.)

'My gracious!' said Taffy, 'what a lot of noise-pictures we've made,— carp-mouth, carp-tail, and egg! Now make another noise, Daddy.'

'Ssh!' said her Daddy, and frowned to himself, but Taffy was too incited to notice.

'That's quite easy,' she said, scratching on the bark.

'Eh, what?' said her Daddy. 'I meant I was thinking, and didn't want to be disturbed.'

'It's a noise, just the same. It's the noise a snake makes, Daddy, when it is thinking and doesn't want to be disturbed. Let's make the *ssh*-noise a snake. Will this do?' And she drew this. (7.)

'There,' she said. 'That's another s'prise-secret. When you draw a hissy-snake by the door of your little back-cave where you mend the spears, I'll know you're thinking hard; and I'll come in most mousy-quiet. And if you draw it on a tree by the river when you're fishing, I'll know you want me to walk most *most* mousy-quiet, so as not to shake the banks.'

'Perfectly true,' said Tegumai. 'And there's more in this game than you think.

Taffy, dear, I've a notion that your Daddy's daughter has hit upon the finest thing that there ever was since the Tribe of Tegumai took to using shark's teeth instead of flints for their spear-heads. I believe we've found out *the* big secret of the world.'

'Why?' said Taffy, and her eyes shone too with incitement.

'I'll show,' said her Daddy. 'What's water in the Tegumai language?'

'*Ya*, of course, and it means river too—like Wagai-*ya*—the Wagai river.'

'What is bad water that gives you fever if you drink it—black water—swamp-water?'

'*Yo*, of course.'

'Now look,' said her Daddy. 'S'pose you saw this scratched by the side of a pool in the beaver-swamp?' And he drew this. (8.)

'Carp-tail and round egg. Two noises mixed! *Yo*, bad water,' said Taffy. ''Course I wouldn't drink that water because I'd know you said it was bad.'

The story you have just read, and the illustration above are taken from an early edition of Kipling's book. In the illustration, you can see a drawing of a tusk with pictures carved on it, showing episodes from the story. Around the tusk, there is some writing. If you can work out which signs resemble modern letters of the alphabet, you can decipher it.

28

Unit 5
Choosing between writing and talking

We have looked at how we use our bodies to communicate with other people and at how useful it is to be able to write.

There are times when we don't need to speak. Our bodies and faces say everything for us. Do you remember the photograph of the girl sticking out her tongue?

Or we may want to communicate by writing; that's why alphabets and writing systems have developed.

Here is a story about Louis the swan who couldn't speak and tried to communicate by writing. Read it in your groups.

Louis worked very hard and learned how to read and write, but all his efforts were in vain.

Louis goes to school by E. B. White

Next morning, Sam took Louis to school with him. Sam rode his pony, and Louis flew along. At the schoolhouse, the other children were amazed to see this great bird, with his long neck, bright eyes, and big feet. Sam introduced him to the teacher of the first grade, Mrs. Hammerbotham, who was short and fat. Sam explained that Louis wanted to read and write because he was unable to make any sound with his throat.

Mrs. Hammerbotham stared at Louis. Then she shook her head. 'No birds!' she said. 'I've got enough trouble.'

Sam looked disappointed.

'Please, Mrs. Hammerbotham,' he said. 'Please let him stand in your class and learn to read and write.'

'Why does a bird need to read and write?' replied the teacher. 'Only *people* need to communicate with one another.'

'That's not quite true, Mrs. Hammerbotham,' said Sam, if you'll excuse me for saying so. I have watched birds and animals a great deal. All birds and animals talk to one another—they really have to, in order to get along. Mothers have to talk to their young. Males have to talk to females, particularly in the spring of the year when they are in love.'

'In *love*?' said Mrs. Hammerbotham, who seemed to perk up at this suggestion. 'What do you know about love?'

Sam blushed.

'What kind of a bird *is* he?' she asked.

'He's a young Trumpeter Swan,' said Sam. 'Right now he's sort of a dirty grey colour, but in another year he'll be the most beautiful thing you ever saw—pure white, with black bill and black feet. He was hatched last spring in Canada and now lives in the Red Rock Lakes, but he can't say ko-hoh the way the other swans can, and this puts him at a terrible disadvantage.'

'Why?' asked the teacher.

'Because it does,' said Sam. 'If *you* wanted to say ko-hoh and couldn't make a single solitary sound, wouldn't *you* feel worried?'

'I don't *want* to say ko-hoh,' replied the teacher. 'I don't even know what it means. Anyway, this is all just foolishness, Sam. What makes you think a bird can learn to read and write? It's impossible.'

'Give him a chance!' pleaded Sam. 'He is well behaved, and he's bright, and he's got this very serious speech defect.'

'What's his name?'

'I don't know,' replied Sam.

'Well,' said Mrs. Hammerbotham. 'if he's coming into my class, he's got to have a name.'

'Maybe we can find out what it is.' She looked at the bird. 'Is your name Joe?'

Louis shook his head.

'Jonathan?'

Louis shook his head.

'Donald?'

Louis shook his head again.

'Is your name Louis?' asked Mrs. Hammerbotham. Louis nodded his head very hard and jumped up and down and flapped his wings.

'Great Caesar's ghost!' cried the teacher. 'Look at those wings! Well, his name is Louis—that's for sure. All right, Louis, you may join the class. Stand right here by the blackboard. And don't mess up the room, either! If you need to go outdoors for any reason, raise one wing.'

Louis nodded. The first-graders cheered. They liked the looks of the new pupil and were eager to see what he could do.

'Quiet, children!' said Mrs. Hammerbotham sternly. 'We'll start with the letter *A*.'

She picked up a piece of chalk and made a big **A** on the blackboard. 'Now *you* try it, Louis!'

Louis grabbed a piece of chalk in his bill and drew a perfect **A** right under the one the teacher had drawn.

'You see?' said Sam. 'He's an unusual bird.'

'Well,' said Mrs. Hammerbotham, '*A* is easy. I'll give him something harder.' She wrote **CAT** on the board. 'Let's see you write *cat*, Louis!'

Louis wrote *cat*.

'Well *cat* is easy, too,' muttered the teacher. '*Cat* is easy because it is short. Can anyone think of a word that is longer than *cat*?'

'Catastrophe,' said Charlie Nelson, who sat in the first row.

'Good!' said Mrs. Hammerbotham. 'That's a good hard word. But does anyone know what it means? What *is* a catastrophe?'

'An earthquake,' said one of the girls.

'Correct!' replied the teacher. 'What else?'

'War is a catastrophe,' said Charlie Nelson.

'Correct!' replied Mrs. Hammerbotham. 'What else is?'

A very small, redheaded girl named Jennie raised her hand.

'Yes, Jennie? What is a catastrophe?'

In a very small, high voice, Jennie said, 'When you get ready to go on a picnic with your father and mother and you make peanut-butter sandwiches and jelly rolls and put them in a thermos box with bananas and an apple and some raisin cookies and paper napkins and some bottles of pop and a few hard-boiled eggs and then you put the thermos box in your car and just as you are starting out it starts to *rain* and your parents say there is no point in having a picnic in the rain, that's a catastrophe.'

'Very good, Jennie,' said Mrs. Hammerbotham. 'It isn't as bad as an earthquake, and it isn't as bad as war. But when a picnic gets called off on account of rain, it *is* a catastrophe for a child, I guess. Anyway, *catastrophe* is a good word. No bird can write *that* word, I'll bet. If I can teach a bird to write *catastrophe*, it'll be big news all over the Sweet

Grass country. I'll get my picture in *Life* magazine. I'll be famous.'

Thinking of all these things, she stepped to the blackboard and wrote **CATASTROPHE**

'O.K., Louis, let's see you write *that*!'

Louis picked up a fresh piece of chalk in his bill. He was scared. He took a good look at the word. 'A long word,' he thought, 'is really no harder than a short one. I'll just copy one letter at a time, and pretty soon it will be finished. Besides, my life is a catastrophe. It's a catastrophe to be without a voice.' Then he began writing **CATASTROPHE** , he wrote, making each letter very neatly. When he got to the last letter, the pupils clapped and stamped their feet and banged on their desks, and one boy quickly made a paper airplane and zoomed it into the air. Mrs. Hammerbotham rapped for order.

'Very good, Louis,' she said. 'Sam, it's time you went to your own classroom—you shouldn't be in my room. Go and join the fifth grade. I'll take care of your friend the swan.'

The story continues like this:

Spring followed winter; summer followed spring. A year went by, and it was springtime again. Still no sign of Louis. Then one morning when Louis's grown-up brothers were playing a game of water polo, one of them looked up and saw a swan approaching in the sky.

'Ko-hoh!' cried the cygnet. He rushed to his father and mother. 'Look! Look! Look!'

All the waterfowl on the lake turned and gazed up at the approaching swan. The swan circled in the sky.

'It's Louis!' said the cob. 'But what is that peculiar little object hanging around his neck by a string? What is that?'

'Wait and see,' said his wife. 'Maybe it's a gift.'

Louis looked down from the sky and spotted what looked like his family. When he was sure, he glided down and skidded to a stop. His mother rushed up and embraced him. His father arched his neck gracefully and raised his wings in greeting. Everyone shouted 'Ko-hoh!' and

'Welcome back, Louis!' His family was overjoyed. He had been gone for a year and a half—almost eighteen months. He looked older and handsomer. His feathers were pure white now, instead of a dirty grey. Hanging by a cord around his neck was a small slate. Attached to the slate by a piece of string was a white chalk pencil.

When the family greetings were over, Louis seized the chalk in his bill and wrote 'Hi, there!' on the slate. He held the slate out eagerly for all to see.

The cob stared at it. The mother swan stared at it. The cygnets stared at it. They just stared and stared. Words on a slate meant nothing to them. They couldn't read. None of the members of his family had ever seen a slate before, or a piece of chalk. Louis's attempt to greet his family was a failure. He felt as though he had wasted a year and a half by going to school and learning to write. He felt keenly disappointed.

And, of course, he was unable to speak. The words on the slate were all he could offer by way of greeting.

Finally his father, the cob, spoke up.

'Louis, my son,' he began in his deep, resonant voice, 'this is the day we have long awaited—the day of your return to our sanctuary in the Red Rock Lakes. No one can imagine the extent of our joy or the depth of our emotion at seeing you again, you who have been absent from our midst for so long, in lands we know not of, in pursuits we can only guess at. How good it is to see your countenance again! We hope you have enjoyed good health during your long absence, in lands we know not of, in pursuits we can only guess at—'

'You've said that once already,' said his wife. 'You're repeating yourself. Louis must be tired after his trip, no matter where he's been or what he's been up to.'

'Very true,' said the cob. 'But I must prolong my welcoming remarks a bit longer, for my curiosity is aroused by that odd little object Louis is wearing around his neck and by the strange symbols he has placed upon it by rubbing that white thing up and down and leaving those strange white tracings.'

'Well,' said Louis's mother, 'we're *all* interested in it, naturally. But Louis can't explain it because he is defective and can't talk. So we'll just have to forget our curiosity for the moment and let Louis take a bath and have dinner.'

Everyone agreed this was a good idea.

Louis swam to the shore, placed his slate and his chalk pencil under a bush, and took a bath. When he was through, he dipped the end of one wing in the water and sorrowfully rubbed out the words 'Hi, there!' Then he hung the slate around his neck again.

Discuss the story in your groups. You might like to consider these points.

● Look at the section where Sam explains to the teacher why birds need to talk to each other. Can you think of any other situations in which they need to communicate? Make your own list of times when birds need to communicate. See if you can add to this list by looking at books on birds from your library.

● Louis' mother thinks that Louis 'is defective and can't talk'. She assumes that because he can't speak, he must be stupid. The whole family are only mildly curious about the 'strange white tracings', the letters he produces.

It never crosses their minds that Louis might be trying to communicate with them, does it?

It might help you to think about this if you wrote a story or acted out your own play.

Imagine that you are a highly intelligent, highly trained astronaut who has been sent as an ambassador to another planet. Your researchers tell you that there may well be life on the planet and, when you get there, you find that there is a race of intelligent beings. They obviously communicate with each other but you cannot understand how they do it.

How do they react to you?

Do they assume you are stupid?

How can you get to communicate with them?

● We are luckier than Louis. We can choose whether to write or talk. Make a list of the times when it is better to write than to talk, and of the times when it is better to talk than to write. Compare your lists with those made by other groups.

You might disagree about some situations. Would writing be better than talking when:

(a) Your teachers want to tell your parents about your progress at school?

(b) You want to complain to the manager of a shop because the shoes you have recently bought are faulty?

(c) You need to apologise to someone?

(d) You want to explain to someone how to find your house?

(e) You want to persuade your headteacher that your school ought to have a tuck-shop or a regular disco?

(f) You want to think through and sort out for yourself some new topic you have just started in maths or geography?

Unit 6
The difference between writing and talking

Talking and writing are very different ways of communicating. We looked in the last unit at times when we might choose one way and not the other.

We do not only use them at different times, but we also use a very different kind of language when we are talking from that which we use when we are writing.

Here are two passages on the same subject. The first is spoken and recorded (the oblique lines/indicate pauses). The second is a written composition. They were both produced by an eleven-year-old girl.

The Pyrenean mountain dog (spoken)
this dog that I'm going to tell you about/lives along our lane/he's huge/and it has/long white hair coming over its face/and/its face is all squashed/as if someone had pushed it in/this dog's a Pyrenean mountain dog/it's very interesting the way the people who have it now/came to get it/you see/they read in the paper/that/this dog/had killed two alsatians/and the magistrate said it had to be destroyed/and they went up to the magistrate in court/and pleaded for it/and said/we live in the country/and/not many people come out there/so we'd be able to keep it/and so/that's what they did/all the same/this dog still has/still has a reputation/for being fierce/my mother and I once went collecting for charity at their house/and/when we went to the back door/we saw this dog/tied up on a piece of string/and/we never went collecting for charity again there [laughs] I hadn't/I hadn't seen this dog for quite a time/and so/even though I wouldn't walk past the house/I'd enough courage to go past it on my bike/and one day as I was cycling along the lane/I came round a corner/and there was the Pyrenean mountain dog/even larger than it had ever seemed to me before/and I didn't know whether to go past it or not/until I noticed that

its owner was there/so/I went up to him/on my bike/and I said, 'It won't hurt or bite will it?'/and he said, 'Oh no, it's too slow now'/I felt very sad/because/it was so very old/and/often it would keep falling down in front of him/and he'd have to/help it up/and pull it up.

The 'Polar Bear' (written)
The 'Polar Bear' is a huge dominating Pyrenean mountain dog. It has a huge, ugly, squashed looking face which is covered by long white hairs. It lives down our lane most unfortunately and has a strange story behind it.

The people who have it now read in the newspapers that this dog had attacked and killed two alsatians, and therefore by order of the magistrate it had to be destroyed. The couple pleaded for it, and were allowed to keep it on the condition they kept it quiet.

However the 'Polar Bear' still has a bad reputation. One day my mother and I were collecting for charity and decided to go to their house. As we walked around the back we saw the dog tied up on what seemed like a piece of string. We never went charity collecting there again.

I had not seen the dog for some time and I could usually pluck up courage to go past their house on my bicycle. One day as I was along the lane I saw from a distance the 'Polar Bear' and, just as I was about to turn back, I noticed it had its owner with it. So I cycled on. As I drew near I asked, 'Will it hurt?' 'No dear it's too old and slow.' It was then I noticed how slow it was, in fact painfully so. I felt then and still do feel very sad because it seems cruel to keep it alive.

● In your groups discuss the differences between the transcript of the talk and the written composition.

You might like to discuss the following points.

1 The talk is longer. Does it give any more information than the composition? What makes it longer?

2 Are there any expressions, or groups of words, in the transcript which you would not expect to see in a piece of writing? Why would you not see them, or use them yourself in a piece of writing?

3 The lines (/) in the transcript show where the girl paused. Can you see any connection between them and any punctuation marks that we might use in writing?

4 Which piece did you enjoy reading most? Why?

● Now make your own comparison.

1 First write your own talk about your favourite book. We all have a favourite book. It might be one you have just read or it might be one that you read or had read to you as a small child. You will be doing some interviews about this later.

When you talk about it, you should quickly sum up the plot, talk about your favourite characters, describe any particularly exciting or moving episodes and explain why you found the book enjoyable.

The talk should last about two minutes. Write down every word you are going to say and then read the prepared talk on to tape.

2 Play back the tape to your group and record the discussion which follows.

3 Discuss how you could tell that the talk was a prepared one which you had read on to tape. In what ways did it not sound 'natural'?

4 Play back the tape of the discussion. In what ways did the language in the discussion differ from that in the prepared talk?

Did you speak in full sentences in the talk? Did everyone use full sentences in the discussion?

Did you use 'fillers'—words like 'um', 'er', 'you know', 'you see' in the talk? In the discussion?

Did you ever start a sentence all over again in the talk? In the discussion?

Did you repeat yourself in the talk? In the discussion?

Unit 7
Using sentences in writing

In the last unit, we looked at some of the differences between speaking and writing. We could summarise the discussions like this:

Speaking	Writing
We don't always use full sentences.	We usually do.
We repeat ourselves.	We rarely do.
We often start sentences again if they don't seem to be working out.	We cross them out and rewrite. They don't appear in final versions.
We use fillers like 'um', 'er', 'you know'.	We only use them when we write dialogue.
We use more words.	We use fewer words.

Now let's look at sentences. We will start with a transcript again.

J: My, well, dad, well we went and just brought the dog home, we didn't know anything about it and, you know, he said, look and I just thought it was going to be . . . and mum didn't let me go straight in she just said, now tell me what dad's brought in there and I thought it was a rabbit because you saw its white legs going like that when I opened the door.
S: Puppies.
J: Carol says to dad, whatever did you bring that home for and she picks it up and says, Ah isn't it lovely (laughter)? My uncle John he's got the brother to it.
S: They're awfully playful when they're puppies but . . .
L: They're a nuisance.
J: My uncle's got another Jack Russell because we've got three Jack Russells in our family.
S: Our labrador was dreadful to train. We

haven't trained it properly now, anyway.
M: When Lassie had puppies, we kind of had to look after them because they were always coming through their fence into our garden.
J: Do you mean Lassie your next door neighbour's dog?
M: Yeah.
J: What about the other one?
S: Well, when our dog had puppies, you know, she was quite old, we thought she might die, she had eight.
J: Eight puppies?
S: Lassie had ten.
L: What put mummy off . . .
J: Our dog's only a little one and he had four, two brown and two black and she's only a small dog really.
L: What put my mum off was that when they're first puppies, when they're first puppies, that's what put my mum off and hearing about all these alsatians mauling children. Mum says whenever you see a dog and it looks a bit vicious, just walk by normal, don't look scared, so whenever I go past Davies's I go walking along . . . (laughter) they've got a great big alsatian, it goes (dog noises).

This is a transcript of a recording of an actual conversation. It is easy enough to understand, isn't it? Look at the two longest sections – they have lines next to them so that you can find them.

We will start with J's story about how she got a puppy. If she was to write that story she would have to make a lot of changes. How would she alter it? She would have to cut out the fillers. She would have to sort out the confusion of 'My, well, dad, well we went and just brought the dog home'. Obviously it was only her dad who brought it home. She did not mean 'we went', but 'he went'. She would have to organise it into sentences. She would have to use quotation marks to help us understand when her dad and mum are speaking.

Let's sort out the words first. Before she could organise the punctuation she would have to cut out words and rearrange them so that they would make sense. If you look on the next page you will see how she might do it.

My, ~~well,~~ dad ~~well, we~~ went and just brought the dog home, we didnt know anything about it ~~and, you know~~, he said, look ~~and~~ I just thought it was going to ~~be~~ _a rabbit_ ~~and~~ mum didn't let me go straight in she just said, now tell me what dad's brought in there ~~and~~ I thought it was a rabbit because _I could see_ ~~you saw~~ its white legs ~~going~~ _moving_ ~~like that~~ when I opened the door.

Did you notice that she would have had to change 'going like that' to 'moving'? Why do you think that is? When she was talking she could use gestures with her hands to show how the puppy's legs were moving. She would wave her hands up and down and say his legs were 'going like that'. Of course we can't do that in writing. We rely on gestures a great deal. Ask your friends to describe a spiral staircase. They will all try to show the shape with their hands.

Once she has sorted out the words, she can decide on the punctuation she will need to help the reader. Her final version might look like this:

My dad just went and brought the dog home. We didn't know anything about it. He said, 'Look'. I just thought it was going to be a rabbit. Mum didn't let me go straight in. She just said, 'Now tell me what dad's brought in there'. I thought it was a rabbit because I could see its white legs moving when I opened the door.

● Now in your groups look at L's long section, at the end of the transcript, the one about alsatians. How would you change it if you were to write it up? First of all rearrange the words. You will need to cut some out, put some in, and rearrange the order in some places. Then sort out the punctuation.

● Next you can use what you have learned here in order to do a class project on favourite books. Do you remember in the last unit you had to give a short talk on your favourite book?

Now you can interview people in your class, your teachers – not just your English teacher, your family and friends about their favourite books. This is what you do:

1 You will need to make up a list of questions to ask all these people. Discuss with your group which questions to use. You will need to explain that you want to know all about people's favourite books and that it doesn't matter how old they were when they read them.

You will need to ask some basic questions, such as:
(a) What is the title of your favourite book?
(b) Who wrote it?
(c) What is it about?
(d) What most impressed you about it?
(e) Was it written for small children, teenagers or adults?

There are many more questions that you could think of. Add some more of your own and write out a list ready for your interviews.

Try asking your questions to two or three people first and then discuss whether your list is full enough or too long.

2 Then interview as many people as possible. You may be able to borrow a tape-recorder to use in school and some of you may have recorders at home that you could use to tape interviews with your family and friends.

3 You will have to take notes during those interviews which you couldn't tape.

4 Listen to your tapes. You will need to write out what people said. You will not have to write out every word, but you will need to play the tape section by section and sort the speech out, as you did with the transcript about dogs, so that you can present the important points which people made in your interviews in written form.

5 You will probably find that there are some books that many people love. Design a cover for these that will give people some idea as to what the book is about and will be attractive enough to make them look inside.

6 You can make a display of your covers and the written up interviews for your classroom or your library. If you did the last unit 'The difference between writing and talking' you should have the talks about your favourite books that you wrote out. Add these to the display.

Unit 8
Making sentences

We all know that written sentences begin with a capital letter and end with a full stop. These are the usual signs we give to readers to show them that a sentence is beginning or ending. Now we are going to look at what happens between the capital letter and the full stop.

Sentences can be as short as one word:

Rubbish.
Help.
Hello.
Goodbye.
Murder.

These are all sentences. They can be a couple of words long:

Get down.
Come here.
I went.
He fell.

They can be much, much longer. Here is a description of Fiver, one of the rabbits in *Watership Down.*

His nose moved continually and when a bumble-bee flew humming to a thistle bloom behind him, he jumped and spun round with a start that sent two nearby rabbits scurrying for holes before the nearest, a buck with black tipped ears, recognized him and returned to feeding.

We can take a very simple sentence and add more and more to it.

He fell.

The boy fell down.
The young boy who had been picking blackberries suddenly slipped and fell down the steep hill.

● Now you try it. Start with a one or two word sentence and keep on adding layers. How long a sentence can your group make?

We can do the same thing in reverse by taking a long sentence and making it shorter. We often do this in making notes.
Look at this sentence:
When I was on my way to school yesterday, I bumped into Reshma who was struggling through the pouring rain weighed down by a huge bag of books which she had been reading for her project on India.
We can shorten this to:
Yesterday I met Reshma.

● Sometimes we deliberately use long sentences when we are trying to talk our way out of trouble. In your groups try and write a really long sentence that you might use to explain to a teacher why you arrived ten minutes late for a lesson. Remember it must only be one sentence. When you have finished, see how short a sentence you can make of it.

Which group made up the best excuse?

Unit 9
Finding patterns in sentences 1

In the last unit we were expanding and contracting sentences – making them longer and shorter. Each group made up two very long sentences and one short one. Each group's set of sentences would have been very different. We could make up thousands and thousands of sentences in our language and they would all be different. But they would all have something in common – they would all have similar patterns.

Look at this nonsense sentence:
Blonky bombledums grunch sloggy hooplers.

It doesn't mean anything, does it? It's nonsense. But you could answer questions about it.

● Try these in your groups:

1 What kind of **bombledums** are they?
2 What is happening to the **hooplers**?
3 What kind of **hooplers** are they?

You can answer them, can't you?

The reason why you can answer the question is that the position of words in a sentence gives us a clue as to what work they must be doing and which other words they must go with.

● Try it out on your group. Think of a sentence in 'real' English and write it out with nonsense words instead of real words. Then write out some questions and see if your friends can get the answers. Don't lose your sentences. You will need to refer to them later.

Let's look again at our first nonsense sentence:
Blonky bombledums grunch sloggy hooplers.

The reason why you could answer questions about it was because you could see that it had the same pattern as a real sentence like:
Big bullies hit small pupils.

Blonky obviously goes with **bombledums** – it describes them like **big** describes **bullies**.

Sloggy obviously goes with **hooplers** like **small** goes with **pupils**.

Grunch is what the bombledums do to the hooplers, like **hit** is what the bullies do to the pupils.

Describing words – we call them *adjectives* – usually go before the word they are describing:
big bullies
small pupils
blonky bombledums
sloggy hooplers

Bullies, pupils, bombledums and hooplers are all *nouns*. One of the ways of checking whether a word is a noun is to see if it will fit a gap like this:
I saw the . . . . yesterday.

Bullies, pupils, bombledums and hooplers would all make sense in the gap, but big, small and other adjectives like red, blonky and sloggy etc. would not.

So adjectives and nouns normally go together and adjectives normally come before nouns. We say: big bullies
                not
                bullies big

That is one pattern that you took for granted when you answered the questions on the nonsense sentence.

● Look at your own nonsense sentence. Did that have any adjectives in it? Make a list of all the nouns and the adjectives which describe them that your group used in its nonsense sentences.

Save your nonsense sentences. You will need them again for the next unit.

Unit 10
Finding patterns in sentences 2

There was another pattern which you took for granted when you answered the questions on the nonsense sentence:
Blonky bombledums grunch sloggy hooplers.

You knew that **blonky** and **sloggy** described the nouns **bombledums** and **hooplers.** But you also knew that the **bombledums grunched** the **hooplers** or that the **hooplers** were being **grunched** by the **bombledums.** You knew that the **bombledums** were doing something and that the poor old **hooplers** were having something done to them.

How did you know that? It was because you knew that the sentence was like:
Big bullies hit small pupils.

You knew that in the English language the order of the sentence tells us who is doing what to whom.

It is very important that we put the words in the right order.
Parrot bites man
means something very different from
Man bites parrot.

There is a pattern that we always use.

These words
grunch
hit
bite
are all *verbs.*

You remember we could check if a word is a noun by asking, 'Will it fill a gap like "I saw the . . . . yesterday"?' One of the ways we can recognise a verb is by seeing if we can change its tense. Can we put it in the present or the past? Take the verb like. It has a present tense – like, and a past tense – liked.

The same is true of the three verbs we have just been looking at:

| *present* | grunch | hit | bite |
| *past* | grunched | hit | bit |

So the pattern is

| *noun* | *verb* | *noun* |

In our nonsense sentence
bombledums   grunch   hooplers
and that must mean that the **bombledums** are doing the **grunching** just as:
Bullies hit **pupils**
means that the **bullies** are doing the **hitting.**

● So go back to your own nonsense sentences. Can you find examples of that pattern?

A sentence normally contains a verb. That is, a word that can change its tense. Try putting in the verbs in this passage. You can use any verb that will fit in with the meaning. Write down your verbs in a list.

Once upon a time there _____ a young princess.
She _____ a very boring life. She _____ her days
sewing, playing the harp, reading tales about
Prince Charmings who _____ to rescue
princesses from curses and dragons. Whenever
she _____ the chance she _____ to the castle
window and _____ the boys practising their
archery and learning how to be splendid
knights.

She _____ angrier and more restless each day
until eventually she _____,

'I _____ tired of being a boring princess. I _____
some fun too. I _____ to learn how to be a
splendid knight.'

She _____ one of the servants to get her a set of
boy's clothes, _____ up her long hair so she
could squash it under a hat and she _____ ready
for adventure.

● Look at your list of verbs. Some of them are
in the present tense. Underline those.

● Now carry on the story for yourself. Continue
to miss out the verbs. Remember you can
check if a word is a verb by trying to put it in
a different tense.

When you finish the story pass it round the
group and see if your friends can guess the
words you have missed out. Remember it
doesn't matter if they guess a different word as
long as it fits in with the meaning.

You will have written some amusing stories.
Perhaps other classes might enjoy trying to
guess the words you missed out.

Choose the best story in your group and see
if you can make it even better. Can you make
the story more exciting or amusing?

● When you have finally polished up the story,
proof-read it (see the unit on 'Proof-reading
your work' that will help you). Check the
spelling and punctuation. Check that anyone
reading it might be able to make a good guess
at the words you have omitted. You can check
this by trying it out on another group. Finally
make a best copy including the passage from
this book which you used to start the story.

You can now offer it to other classes as a
way of learning about verbs and improving
their reading because as you have found, you
have to read very carefully to guess which
word is omitted. Other classes may also learn
new words by having to guess at your words.

Unit 11
Using a dictionary 1

Our language is always changing. There are no really permanent rules about what is correct and what is incorrect. So dictionaries are constantly being revised and changed as new words enter our language, old ones change their meanings and new spellings replace old ones. Let's look at some examples.

New words enter the language. The word 'skateboard' appears in a dictionary published in 1979, but not in one published in 1977. It became widely used between these dates.

Old words change their meanings. The word **awful** originally meant inspiring or producing awe or terror. Now it just means bad – 'That was an awful joke' – or very – 'I waited an awfully long time'.

Spellings alter. **Fantasy** used to be spelt **phantasy**.

A dictionary is like a referee. It interprets the 'rules' of our language as they appear to be at the time the dictionary is compiled, or put together. It tells us about the spelling and meanings of words and records their use. As well as recording unusual or old-fashioned words, a dictionary will show us how new words are used and what they mean.

The first really important dictionary was compiled by Samuel Johnson and published in 1755. Before then there had been no real authority to turn to to check how a word was generally spelt and what it meant to most people at the time.

The dictionary is not the only way of finding out what words mean as you will see in the unit called 'Using context clues'. You can often work out for yourself how a word might be spelt.

The dictionary is a very useful tool once you know how to use it.

How do you find your way round the dictionary?

Let's look at a sample page from *The Oxford Paperback Dictionary*, shown opposite.

The first thing to realise is that all the words are in *alphabetical order*. It is not only the first letter of the word which dictates its position in the dictionary. If you have several words which begin with the same letters, you have to go further and further into each word to find the alphabetical order.

You can see how this works if you look at the first four words.

> **audacious**
>
> **audacious** (aw-**day**-shŭs) *adj.* bold, daring. **audaciously** *adv.*, **audacity** (aw-**dass**-iti) *n.*
> **audible** *adj.* loud enough to be heard. **audibly** *adv.*, **audibility** *n.*
> **audience** *n.* **1.** people who have gathered to hear or watch something. **2.** people within hearing. **3.** a formal interview with a ruler or other important person.
> **audio** *n.* **1.** audible sound reproduced mechanically. **2.** its reproduction. □ **audio typist.** one who types from a recording.

They all begin with **aud**, but you can see how the letters which follow are used to put them in alphabetical order:

audacious
audible

These are in order according to the fourth letter

audience
audio

and here it is the fifth letter that is used to put the words in order.

How do you find the page your word will be on?

This is quite simple. Look at the words in heavy black type at the top of the page from the dictionary. Can you see what they are telling you? The first word on the page is **audacious** and the last word on the page is **autocrat**. They are called **guide words**. They tell you that if the word you are looking for comes between these two, this is the page for you.

audacious (aw-**day**-shŭs) *adj.* bold, daring. **audaciously** *adv.*, **audacity** (aw-**dass**-iti) *n.*

audible *adj.* loud enough to be heard. **audibly** *adv.*, **audibility** *n.*

audience *n.* **1.** people who have gathered to hear or watch something. **2.** people within hearing. **3.** a formal interview with a ruler or other important person.

audio *n.* **1.** audible sound reproduced mechanically. **2.** its reproduction. □ **audio typist**, one who types from a recording.

audio-visual *adj.* (of teaching aids etc.) using both sight and sound.

audit *n.* an official examination of accounts to see that they are in order. —*v.* to make an audit of.

audition *n.* a trial to test the ability of a prospective performer. —*v.* **1.** to hold an audition. **2.** to be tested in an audition.

auditor *n.* a person who makes an audit.

auditorium (awdit-**or**-iŭm) *n.* the part of a building in which an audience sits.

auger (**awg**-er) *n.* a tool for boring holes in wood, like a gimlet but larger.

aught (*pr.* awt) *n.* (*old use*) anything, *for aught I know.*

augment (awg-**ment**) *v.* to add to, to increase. **augmentation** *n.*

au gratin (oh **grat**-an) cooked with a crisp crust of breadcrumbs or grated cheese.

augur (**awg**-er) *v.* to foretell, to be a sign of; *this augurs well for your future,* is a favourable sign.

august (aw-**gust**) *adj.* majestic, imposing.

August *n.* the eighth month of the year.

auk *n.* a northern sea-bird with small narrow wings.

auld lang syne days of long ago.

aunt *n.* **1.** a sister or sister-in-law of one's father or mother. **2.** (*children's informal*) an unrelated woman friend, *Aunt Jane.* □ **Aunt Sally**, a figure used as a target in a throwing-game; a target of general abuse or criticism.

auntie *n.* (*informal*) an aunt.

au pair (oh **pair**) a young woman from overseas helping with housework and receiving board and lodging in return.

aura (**or**-ă) *n.* the atmosphere surrounding a person or thing and thought to come from him or it, *an aura of happiness.*

aural (**or**-ăl) *adj.* of the ear. **aurally** *adv.*

au revoir (oh rĕ-**vwahr**) goodbye for the moment.

aurora (aw-**ror**-ă) *n.* bands of coloured light appearing in the sky at night and probably caused by electrical radiation from the North and South magnetic poles. **aurora borealis** (bor-i-**ay**-lis), also called

the Northern Lights, in the northern hemisphere. **aurora australis**, in the southern hemisphere.

auspicious (aw-**spish**-ŭs) *adj.* showing signs that promise success. **auspiciously** *adv.*

Aussie (**oz**-i) *n.* (*informal*) an Australian.

austere (aw-**steer**) *adj.* severely simple and plain, without ornament or comfort. **austerely** *adv.*

austerity (aw-**ste**-riti) *n.* being austere, an austere condition, *the austerities of life in wartime.*

Australasia (oss-trăl-**ay**-shă) Australia, New Zealand, and neighbouring islands in the South Pacific. **Australasian** *adj. & n.*

Australia (oss-**tray**-liă) a continent between the Pacific and Indian Oceans. **Australian** *adj. & n.*

Austria (**oss**-stri-ă) a country in Europe. **Austrian** *adj. & n.*

authentic *adj.* genuine, known to be true. **authentically** *adv.*, **authenticity** *n.*

authenticate *v.* to prove the truth or authenticity of. **authentication** *n.*

author *n.* **1.** the writer of a book or books etc. **2.** the originator of a plan or policy. **authoress** *n.*, **authorship** *n.*

authoritarian (awth-o-ri-**tair**-iăn) *adj.* favouring complete obedience to authority as opposed to individual freedom. —*n.* a supporter of such principles.

authoritative (awth-o-ri-tă-tiv) *adj.* having or using authority. **authoritatively** *adv.*

authority *n.* **1.** the power or right to give orders and make others obey, or to take specific action. **2.** a person or group with such power. **3.** a person with specialized knowledge, a book etc. that can supply reliable information, *he is an authority on spiders.*

authorize *v.* **1.** to give authority to. **2.** to give authority for, to sanction, *I authorized this payment.* **authorization** *n.* □ **Authorized Version**, the English translation of the Bible (1611) made by order of King James I and appointed to be read in churches.

autistic (aw-**tiss**-tik) *adj.* having a form of mental illness that causes a person to withdraw into a private world of fantasy and be unable to communicate with others or respond to his real environment, *autistic children.* **autism** (**aw**-tizm) *n.* this condition.

autobiography *n.* the story of a person's life written by himself. **autobiographical** *adj.*

autocracy (aw-**tok**-răsi) *n.* despotism.

autocrat (**aw**-tŏ-krat) *n.* a person with unlimited power, a dictatorial person.

37

43

What if you can't spell a word?

How do you find it? You make an intelligent guess at how it might be spelt. Take the word **auk** – a sea bird. If you did not know how to spell it, you could make several guesses. It could be **awk** – like the beginning of awkward. It could be **ork** – like the beginning of Orkney. It could be **auk** with the **au** sounding like the beginning of August. All you would need to do would be to check those guesses until you got it right.

● Now try it for yourself. You can work individually, or in groups, but you will need your own dictionary.

Using guide words.
How quickly can you find these words by using the guide words? Write down the guide words of the page you found them on.
regardless
headstone
cramped

Understanding alphabetical order.
Put the following words into alphabetical order:
rifle rice ribbon ride rich
succeed substitute suburban successor
subtraction

Making intelligent guesses.
If you did not know how to spell these words, what guesses would you make about how they might be spelt and why?
flirt idle dairy moan ache

44

Unit 12
Using a dictionary 2

Dictionaries do not only tell us what words mean and how they are spelt. They give us much more information.

Look again at the page from the *Oxford Paperback Dictionary*. It tells us: how words are pronounced; how words are used; and gives us other forms of the word.

1 How some words are pronounced

Before you can use the pronunciation guides you need to understand two things:
(a) Words are made up of *syllables*. A syllable is a unit of sound. For example, take the word **audience**. It has three syllables: **aud**-i-ence. The word **table** has two syllables: **tab**-le. The word **can** has only one syllable.
(b) When a word has more than one syllable, we stress or emphasise one of them more than the other or others. For example we stress the syllable **class** in the word **class**room, and we stress the syllable **ap** in **ap**ple.

Look at the dictionary entry for **Aussie**. The guide to pronunciation comes in brackets immediately after the word like this:
Aussie (**oz**–i)
It tells us that there are two syllables; **oz** is in heavy black type, that means that we emphasise or stress that syllable.
Now look at the entry for **audacious**. Here we get
audacious (aw–**day**–shus)
So we know that there are three syllables and we stress the middle one.

● Talk it through in your groups. Here are some points to consider.

(i) Look at the pronunciation guides on the page from the *Oxford Paperback Dictionary*. Try to say the words out loud.
(ii) Have you understood syllables? How many syllables are there in: author, sofa, Jamaica, England?
(iii) Have you understood stress? Which syllables do we stress in: Australia, science, curry, homework?
(iv) This dictionary gives pronunciation guides to some words only. Why do you think that is?
(v) The dictionary that you use in class, or your own dictionary, may use a different system for showing how to pronounce a word. Can you work it out?

2 How some words are used

(a) Informal use
Look at the entries for auntie and Aussie They are:
auntie *n. (informal)* an aunt
Aussie (**oz**–i) *n. (informal)* an Australian
The word **informal** tells us that we use these words in everyday speech, but that they are not used when we are writing or speaking formally.

It's rather like slang which we use in some situations and not in others. We look at this in more detail in the next unit and in the unit called 'Using standard English'.

(b) Old use
Sometimes in your reading, you will come across words which we no longer use in modern English. The dictionary records them as well as words we use now. Look at the entry for **aught**.

aught (*pr.* awt) *n. (old use)* anything, *for aught I know*

The first item (*pr.* awt) is the pronunciation guide. Why is it different from the ones we looked at earlier? The last item *for aught I know* is useful because it gives an example of how the word was used.

(c) Use with other words

The *Oxford Paperback Dictionary* uses a special symbol □ to mean; 'here comes an example of how the word can combine with other words and maybe change its original meaning'. Look at the entry for **aunt**.

Aunt *n.* **1.** a sister or sister-in-law of one's father or mother. **2.** (*children's informal*) an unrelated woman friend, Aunt Jane.
□ **Aunt Sally**, a figure used as a target in a throwing game; a target of general abuse or criticism.

You can see similar examples if you look at the entries for **audio** and **authorize**.

● Talk it through in your groups
(i) What about these *informal* words? We will look at how you change your language, the way you speak and write, in different situations in the unit called 'Using standard English'. For now, make a list of some of the slang words you and your group use and see if you can find them in the dictionary. You probably won't find very many. Why do you think that is? Keep the list. You will need it for the next unit 'Making your own dictionary'.
(ii) Why do you think the dictionary gives us old-fashioned words like 'aught' if no one uses them any more?
(iii) By adding one word to another, we often change the meaning of the first word or of both words. For example if we start with the word ball and then add boy we change the meaning of the first word. Here are some more examples:
bunny + girl = bunny girl
coffee + cup = coffee cup
Can you think of some examples of your own?

3 *Other forms of the word*

Look at the entry for **audible**. We are given two other words **audibly** and **audibility**. Words often change their endings depending on how we want to use them. Take a simple word like beauty. You could say
She had great beauty
or
She was very beautiful
or
She dressed beautifully
You could do the same with these words.
You could say
The audibility of her voice was poor
or
Her voice was hardly audible
or
She did not speak audibly.

The dictionary gives abbreviations with these words:

adj.	= adjective	*n.*	= noun
adv.	= adverb	*v.*	= verb

The only word you might not know here is *adverb*. An adverb describes a verb as an adjective describes a noun. Here are some examples:
Susan ran *slowly*
Slowly is an adverb, it describes how she ran.
The dog ate *quickly*
Quickly tells us how the dog ate – it describes the verb ate.
An adverb also gives more information about an adjective.

The	large	book
	adjective	*noun*

can become

The	*very*	large	book
	adverb	*adjective*	*noun*

or

The *extremely*	large book
The *impressively*	large book
The *fairly*	large book
The *really*	large book

All the words in italics are adverbs. They describe the adjective 'large'.

Unit 13
Making your own dictionary

In some of the units that follow you will be asked to gather lists of words so that individually, or in groups, or as a class you can make your own dictionaries of:
(a) new words which have recently entered our language like skateboard or hang-glide
(b) words which you find in one dialect and not in others
(c) words we have borrowed from other languages
(d) American words like garbage and sidewalk that we understand, but do not often use
(e) special words to do with school.

● You have already made a list of some slang words that you know. Can you make your own dictionary of slang? Before you start you will have to be quite sure what slang is. Discuss in your groups what you mean by the word.

● Here are some ideas for you to discuss before you define the word.

1 Slang is something we only use with people we know well or have something in common with. Take a sentence like
'I like that record.'
How many other ways can you think of for saying that?
You might say it just like that to someone who was older than you, but what would you say to a friend in your class? Jot down the words you would use.

2 The slang which one group of people use is sometimes difficult for another group to understand. Do you use slang words which your parents or teachers don't understand? What are they? Write them down.

3 Slang rapidly goes out of fashion. Ask people older than you what slang words they used to mean that they liked something. You will probably find a huge variety of words – some examples are *cool, swinging, super, ace.* What words are in fashion now? Make a list of them.

4 People often disapprove of slang. Why do you think that is? Have you ever been told not to use it? By whom? Samuel Johnson didn't include the word in his 1755 dictionary, but Webster's dictionary of 1828 includes it. It is defined as 'low vulgar un-meaning language'. Do you agree? Do you enjoy using it?

5 Here are some examples of slang words and phrases. Can you add your own? Make a note of them.
head –
    Shakespeare uses several slang expressions for this word:
    costard (means apple)
    mazard (means bowl)
    scance (means lantern)
policeman –
    copper   fuzz
    bobby   cops
    peeler (this was used in Victorian times)
money –
    bread   dough
    cash   ackers
    lucre   greenies
nonsense –
    rot
    bunkum
    tripe
go away –
    buzz off   hop it   get on your bike
    clear off   scran   sling your hook

6 What slang words do you use for these?
cigarette   girl friend
truanting   lavatory
boy friend
Make a note of them.

When you have discussed these points, try to write your own definition of slang in your group. Compare your group's definition with those used by other groups.

● By now you should have quite a long list of slang words and expressions and you are ready to start compiling your own dictionary of slang There may be a dictionary of slang in your school library. Have a look at it. You will find it very interesting and it will help you decide how to set out your own dictionary. You could make the dictionary individually, in groups or as a class. You will need to set it out professionally. So you will need:

1 To put the words in a new order. You have collected lists under different headings; slang words for head, police, money etc. You will need to put them into strict alphabetical order now. Leave plenty of space between words so that you can add new ones as you think of them.

2 To use guide words at the top of your page so you can find words quickly.

3 To give a guide to pronunciation.

4 To give some advice as to how the expression should be used. It would be a good idea to put the word into a sentence to show how it is used.

5 To show other forms of the word. For example the noun 'copper' (policeman) can become a verb 'cop' as in 'He was copped for it'.

You should compile this dictionary in a loose-leaf folder because there will be other sections to add to it as you work through the next units.

Keep your own personal dictionary

This is very useful. You should keep a notebook divided into alphabetical sections in which you write down:

1 Words you know you have difficulty in spelling. It only takes a moment to check the correct version in your own dictionary.

2 New words you meet. You are introduced to new words all the time at school. Every subject has its own vocabulary. You will often need a guide to pronunciation and meaning because, for example, the word 'reflex' has a meaning in mathematics that it doesn't always have in other situations.

3 Words you enjoy using or words you have come across in your reading which you want to use in future. Again you will need a guide to pronunciation, meaning and how the words can be used.

Unit 14
How English grew

The English language is forever changing and developing. Every tribe or nation that invaded us left a legacy of new words in our language. Every country that traded with us gave us new words. From every country we visited, fought or traded with we brought back new words. As you saw in the unit 'Using a dictionary 1' new words are constantly coming into our language.

Here are some 'good old English' words and the languages we got them from.

alphabet – Greek
The first two letters in the Greek alphabet are *alpha* – our 'A', and *beta* – our 'B'. Put them together and you have the word 'alphabet'.

fan – Latin
A football fan is a supporter of a team. The word comes from the Latin word *fanum* meaning a temple. Someone who was constantly in the temple was called a 'fanatic'.

So anyone who is an enthusiast for something is now called a fan.

daisy – Saxon
The daisy looks like a sun surrounded by petals; since the sun is the eye of the day the Saxons called it the *daeges eage* – the day's eye.

orange – Arabic
The word in Arabic is *naranj*. At first people ate a naranj. Listen to the sound and you will understand how it became an orange.

alligator – Spanish
The word was *el lagarto* meaning the lizard.

khaki – Urdu
The Urdu word for dust is *khak*. From this we get the name khaki given to dust-coloured uniforms.

thug – Hindu
The word *thug* in Hindu means a member of a band of robbers and murderers. It has much the same meaning for us.

All these are part of what we now call the 'Queen's English'.

Other countries steal from us too. The French now talk about *le weekend* and *le picnic*, *le blue jeans* and *le football*!

Here are some more words which we have borrowed.

cargo	dungarees	tomato
guerrilla	whisky	chocolate
vodka	pyjamas	balcony
sherbet	juggernaut	incognito
arsenal	cot	hamburger
mattress	kiosk	typhoon
sofa	tea	poodle
alcohol	café	curry

In your groups choose four words each and see if you can find where they have come from. A dictionary like the *Concise Oxford* will help. There is a section at the very end of the definition in brackets that will tell you. For example, the entry for 'camel' has this at the very end:

(c.f. Heb gamal camel, Arab Jamala carry)

(c.f.	Heb	gamal	camel,
compare with	Hebrew	the Hebrew word	this is what it means
	Arab	Jamala	carry)
	Arabic	the Arabic word	this is what it means

Can you think of any words which are borrowed from other languages? It may be that there are people in your class who speak more than one language. Ask them about words they know in their language that are also in English.

● The first thing to do is to find out what other languages are known by members of your class. Perhaps one group could find this out. You will need to conduct a survey. These are some of the questions you will need to ask everyone:

1 Do you speak a language other than English? What is it?

2 Do you understand but not speak a language other than English? What is it?

3 Do you speak or understand a third language? What is it?

Once you have made your checklist of languages in your class, you can then ask all those people who use one or more other languages if there are words in those languages that are also in English.

● In the last unit you started your own dictionary. Now you can add another section to it: You can call it 'Words English has borrowed from languages used in our class.' Make headings under the different languages and enter borrowed words alphabetically under each heading. Leave plenty of space to enter new words as people notice or remember them.

Remember to add pronunciation guides and guides to the meaning where necessary.

You can go on adding to this dictionary. The next sections will look at dialects and the language of school and you will be adding a new section to your dictionary for each of them.

● You may find that there are many languages used by people in your class. You could make a display for the classroom wall so that other people could see what you have discovered. You could list the languages and put the borrowed words next to them.

Unit 15
Is there only one English?

We have seen that English is a mongrel language; it borrows new words to suit its purposes. We will look at other ways it has changed and is changing in the unit called 'Our changing language'.

It is also a very popular language. More people can speak English than any other language. In fact, three-quarters of the world's business mail is estimated to be written in English. Over 300 million people speak it as a first, second or third language. The way they speak it varies enormously. Even within the British Isles there is great variety in the way English is spoken. Think of someone from Glasgow talking to someone from Cornwall and you will see how the language changes from place to place.

Everyone who speaks English speaks with an *accent* or a *dialect*. What are these?
An accent is a particular way of pronouncing words. For example: someone from the south-east of England will say the word bath as if it rhymed with hearth, while someone in the north will pronounce the word as if it rhymed with the girl's name Kath. We all have accents and we also have dialects.
A dialect is also a particular way of pronouncing words, but it has two other features:

1 *Many dialects have their own special words* which only crop up in that dialect. Dialects, like accents, often reflect the language of a particular part of the country so we can look at some local examples.

Someone from Yorkshire might enjoy a toasted, buttered *pikelet* at tea time; a Londoner would enjoy it just as much, but would call it a *crumpet*.

Pupils in Bristol wear *daps* for gym; pupils in Teesside wear the same things and call them *pumps*.

Boys in Devon refer to the girls in their class as *maids*. In Sheffield they call them *lasses*.

2 *Sometimes dialects have different kinds of grammatical constructions.* A Scottish person might ask,
'What like is it in Devon?'
To which a Devonian could reply,
'It be cold and raining.'
Here are some examples of a Suffolk dialect which has its own grammatical rules.

Us don't want t'play wi'he.
Oi don't think much o'they.

There is a dialect that we are all familiar with. It is called *standard English*. Sometimes it is referred to as 'Queen's English', 'BBC English' or 'proper English'. In fact it is no more proper or improper than any other dialect. It has its own *grammar* just like the Devon dialect; the standard English version of the reply about the weather would be, 'It's cold and raining.'

It has its own *vocabulary* only, unlike local dialects, its words are more generally understood. For example a northern dialect may call a child 'mardy' and standard English dialect would call him 'sulky'.

It has its own *accent*. The accent is called Received Pronunciation. BBC news readers generally, but not always, have that accent. Some people call it 'talking posh'. A better way of defining it would be to say that it is the accent which gives no clues about where the speaker has lived.

● Here are some examples of dialects other than standard English. In your groups, or individually, rewrite them in standard English.
You will notice that the spelling sometimes has to change so that the writer can help you hear the accent. You will have to change it

back to standard spelling. You will need to change the grammar too. There are also some dialect words that you may not know. Can you guess from the rest of the passage what they mean?

As you discuss how to rewrite the extracts you should also consider how much interest and liveliness they lose when you try to change them into standard English. In each case, try to guess where the dialect is from.

The first piece is a traditional poem.

Biby
A muvver was barfin 'er biby one night,
The youngest of ten and a tiny young mite,
The muvver was poor and the baby was thin,
Only a skelington covered in skin;
The muvver turned rahnd for the soap orf the
    rack,
She was but a moment but when she turned
    back,
The biby was gorn; and in anguish she cried,
Oh, where is my biby? – The angels replied:

Your biby 'as fell dahn the plug-hole,
Your biby 'as gorn dahn the plug;
The poor little thing was so skinny and thin
E 'oughter been barfed in a jug;
Your biby is perfectly 'appy,
'E won't need a barf any more;
Your biby as fell dahn the plug-hole,
Not lost but gorn before!

                                    Anon

In the next piece, two boys are discussing their new headmaster.

'Dat man mek me frighten bad yu know,' Ricky said as we reached the end of the playground and started to pick up the papers. 'A hope me no have fe go ina' im affice, cause de way me 'fraid a dat man bwoy, it's nobody's business,' I replied, more relieved. 'Me sarry fa dem picney 'im hit wid 'im strap,' Ricky teased. 'Bwoy dem dey picney can't sit down fa weeks yu know.'

The last piece is another conversation between two boys.

'Where were you yesterday, then, Marshall? Wagging off?'
'I went down to t'farm.'
'Tha's barmy about them animals, isn't tha?'
'Specially pigs.'
'I'd better say nowt about them. Else I know
    tha'll thump me.'

In the last unit, we looked at how you might go about finding out how many languages were used by the people in your class. There are probably many different dialects too. You could start to build up a class tape-library of all your different dialects.

● Ask people to tell a joke or story on tape in their ordinary speech.

When you have some tapes you could listen to them in groups and discuss:

1 The ways in which accent, grammar and vocabulary differ.

2 Whether the story or joke would have been so interesting if it were told in Received Pronunciation, or with the vocabulary and grammar of standard English. What would it lose?

Unit 16
Our changing language

The English language is always changing, and always has been. Caxton, the early printer, found it a great problem. Here is the prologue, or opening section, of his book *Eneydos*. He is worried that one person calls the things that hens lay, and you and I have for breakfast, *egges* and another person might call them *eyren*. He is confused as to what word he should print so that everyone could understand. This prologue was written in 1490. You can see how much our spelling has changed since then. In your groups try to translate it. See if you can read the humorous story he is telling. Don't worry if you cannot understand all of it.

And certaynly our langage now vsed varyeth ferre from that whiche was vsed and spoken whan I was borne/For we englysshe men/ben borne vnder the domynacyon of the mone, whiche is neuer stedfaste/but euer wauerynge one season/and waneth & dyscreaseth another season/And that comyn englysshe that is spoken in one shyre varyth from a nother. In so moche that in my dayes happened that certayn marchauntes were in a shippe in tamyse,* for to haue sayled ouer the see into zelande/and for lacke of wynde, thei taryed atte forlond, and wente to lande for to refreshe them; And one of theym named sheffelde, a mercer, cam in-to an hows and exed for mete; and specally he axyd after eggys; And the goode wyf answerde, that she coude speke no frensche. And the marchaunt was angry, for he also coude speke no frensche, but wolde haue hadde egges/and she vnderstode hym not/And thenne at laste a nother sayd that he wolde haue eyren/then the good wyf sayd that she vnderstod him wel/Loo, what sholde a mann in thyse dayes now wryte, egges or eyren/certaynly it is harde to playse euery man/by cause of dyuersite & chaunge of langage.

* Thames

Caxton may have been worried that it was 'hard to please every man', but he was one of the great pioneers of printing and could not see the great effect printing would have on language. He had to decide which dialect word to use, and as people began to learn to read English, they read the words the printer decided to use and gradually some of the dialect words became less common than others, or became used only in a spoken form in their own area and not outside it.

Some occupations had their own special dialect words which remain with us to this day. One of the most interesting examples is the way that some northern shepherds and fishermen count. They use words from the Celtic language that people spoke in that area before the Romans came. Some shepherds still count their sheep like this:

'Yan, teyan, tethera, methera, pip, raise, ceesa, hora, catra, dick, yanna-dick, teyanna-dick, tethera-dick, methera-dick, jigga, raisa-dick, ceesa-dick, hora-dick, catra-dick, bumfa'.

Can you see any similiarities between that counting system and our own? The numbers do not need to go beyond twenty because the shepherd uses a tally stick which he marks each time he comes to twenty and he adds up his final total at the end. Why do you think these words still exist?

Children also have their own separate language which varies from one part of the country to another, and because it has hardly ever been written down, it has remained varied.

● What do you say when you want to stop a game for a moment? Check with your group and then with the whole class. You will probably find a number of words.

Some that are known about are:

kings, creams, creamos, olly-oxalls, olly-olly-ee, double queenie, cross-kings, kings, fingers, pax.

● And what do you say if you want to stake a claim to something? Check this with your group and class too. Make a list of the words you use.

Some words you might use are:

bags, bagsy, bagsy mine, ballow (as in 'I ballows that'), barley (as in 'barley me that'), pike prior pike, squits, lardie.

Sometimes a dialect develops in its own way because the speakers of it are a long way away from people who use standard English.

American English developed like this. The first English settlers went to America in 1620 and in three hundred and fifty-odd years a dialect developed there which is quite different from the ones which developed here. It has a different pronunciation, a different grammar:

American	English
It's real good	It's really good
He has gotten himself a book	He has got himself a book

and a different vocabulary. Look at these words and their translations:

American	English
purse	handbag
sidewalk	pavement
cookie	biscuit
fall	autumn

● In your groups find out the meanings of the following American words:

elevator	overpass
janitor	semester
muffler	recess

An American/English dictionary will help.

Can you think of any more American words which we might not easily understand? Listen out for them the next time you watch an American film or television programme. You will be able to guess their meanings from the context. Add them to your dictionary with the help of your group. You could call this section 'American words we know'.

Sometimes a dialect develops because there is a reason for not speaking standard English. This is one of the possible reasons for the growth of Cockney rhyming slang. It developed in East London and was useful in that outsiders could not crack the codes it used. Have you ever used a code language? You might have used pig Latin or back slang or some other code to talk or write to your friends in if you did not want others to know what was going on. We will look in more detail at that later in book two of this series. Here are some examples of Cockney rhyming slang:

Sweeny Todd	Flying Squad
Auntie Ella	umbrella
boat race	face
boracic lint	skint (broke)
butcher's hook	look
Duchess of Fife	wife
frog and toad	road
whistle and flute	suit
Uncle Bert	shirt

Only the first word of the rhyme is used so the meaning is doubly hidden. Here is an example:

Take a butchers at me new whistle and uncle. I ain't 'arf boracic now. Lord knows what me old Duch will say. I can't wait to see 'er boat when I come down the frog.'

● Can you translate this? Here are some more words. Make up your sentences with words from either list.

Andy Cain	rain
cash and carried	married
daisy roots	boots
elephant's trunk	drunk
rabbit and pork	talk
plates of meat	feet
Hampstead Heath	teeth

Now make up your own rhyming slang just within your groups, and then try out some sentences on the whole class.

● Now you can add another section to your dictionary: 'Dialect words we use'. Gather together the words that you know are used in the dialects used in your class which are not in standard English. You will already have thought of some when you looked at the words you used to stop a game or stake a claim to something, but there will be many more. When you have your lists of words discuss the following points:

1 Can you think of a word in standard English that means just the same as your dialect word (like pikelet = crumpet)?

2 If you can't think of a standard English word that fits, there may be a reason why the word only appears in one dialect. Can you think why that should be so?

Unit 17
Using standard English

It is very useful to be able to use standard English when you want to. It does not matter whether you pronounce it with a local accent or whether you use Received Pronunciation, but there are times when you will need to use the vocabulary and grammar of standard English. This is particularly so in the case of writing. We tend to speak our own dialect and write it from time to time, but in the situations outlined below it is valuable to be able to write in standard English.

1 We use that dialect when we communicate with someone outside our immediate area. Local dialects may not easily be understood outside their area. Imagine someone from Glasgow writing to someone from Cornwall. Standard English is the dialect they both understand.

2 It is the dialect we use when we communicate with people outside the circle of our family and friends.

3 It is the dialect used by people who have power. You would write in standard English if you were applying for a job. It is the dialect of the business world, the media; newspapers, television and advertising.

You choose your dialect rather as you choose your clothes to fit the situation. The clothes you enjoy wearing round the house are not the clothes you would feel right in if you were going for an interview for a job or going to an important social occasion.

You can be reasonably sure that you can make yourself understood in standard English and that it will be acceptable in most situations.

It is important to realise that your own dialect is valuable because:

1 Your accent or dialect is part of you, like your finger prints. It declares where you were born and brought up. It tells other people more about you.

2 If you have standard English and another accent or dialect you can choose which to use in which circumstance and which one is most appropriate.

3 We use standard English for written communication, but many people use the words and grammar of standard English without using Received Pronunciation. That is the accent that goes with the dialect. The BBC, which used to insist that all its newsreaders used Received Pronunciation, often has readers with local accents now.

4 You can often write and speak more vividly if you use your own dialect.

● Everybody's language changes according to circumstances. In your groups discuss the following questions:

1 Do you use the same accent, words and grammar when you are speaking to:
(a) your grandmother?
(b) your teacher?
(c) your friends?
(d) someone you have only just met?
(e) someone you want to impress?
(f) someone who knows you well?
(g) on the telephone?

2 Do you write the same kind of English when you:
(a) write a note to the milkman?
(b) write a letter to your friend?
(c) write a letter to your teacher?
(d) write an essay in a history exam?

You will probably find that you use very different forms of English in these situations. Do you think that the conversation with your

teacher is in proper English and the one with your friend is 'improper'? Both of them are equally good. It would be improper to speak to your friends in the reserved, careful way you might speak to your teacher. Your friends would think you had gone mad! This is the kind of difference we looked at briefly in 'Using a dictionary 2' when we looked at the entries for auntie and Aussie which were both followed by (informal).

● Look more closely at how the words and expressions we use can alter according to the situation we are in by writing a story or a play which you could record with some friends. Here are some ideas to get you started.

(a) A scene involving teachers and pupils. The pupils could be talking among themselves when the teacher arrives. How does their language change?

(b) Do you think teachers always talk in the same way? Imagine your teacher describing your class to a friend in the staff room. Would she speak in the same way as she does in the classroom?

(c) 'Don't you speak to me like that!' Have you ever heard anyone say that? Have you ever said it to anyone else? If you have, it was probably to someone younger. Write a story where the situation is reversed. Can you imagine telling off your teacher for forgetting your books?

(d) We often think one thing and say something else. Write a play in which someone is being very polite, or being told off when they are really quite annoyed. Write what they are really thinking in brackets after what they have actually said. If you did this on tape you could use a different tone of voice for the thoughts.

Unit 18
What about proper English?

We have discussed some of the ways in which we might look at the dialect of English called 'standard English'. Some people might wonder if it is more correct or a finer language than any other dialect.

Does it sound better?

Most languages have one dialect which they think is more elegant than any other of its dialects. The strange thing is that people who do not speak the language cannot tell simply from listening which dialect is supposed to be more elegant. A recent experiment was conducted in which French–Canadians who did not know English, listened to tapes of different dialects and were asked to say which was the best. Very few people picked standard English. So it seems that there are no real reasons for saying that one way of speaking is more attractive than another.

Is it more correct?

It is just as correct as any other dialect. Every dialect has its rules about how you make plurals, for example, or how its grammar works. In Jamaican patois (that is the name of the dialect that comes from there) a plural is made by adding 'dem' so
'the boys' becomes 'da boy dem'

In the dialect of south-west England it is possible to say
'I be a farmer'
when standard English would say
'I am a farmer'.

There is no simple rule about what is right or wrong; dialects simply work in different ways. You need to be able to use standard English along with any other dialect you may have and you need to know how its grammar works so that you can use it properly, but its grammar is not necessarily better than that of any other dialect. It is different.

Should we worry about our language changing

Standard English, like every other dialect, is always changing. The **spelling** has changed dramatically – look again at the passage from Caxton on page 53.

The **pronunciation** has changed. In the eighteenth century *tea* would have rhymed with *say*.

The **grammar** has changed. Someone who used standard English in the eighteenth century would say
I ain't

Now a standard English speaker would say 'I am not' and 'I ain't' is used in the London dialect.

● Now some discussion points for you and your groups. Individually you should take one of the following questions as the starting point for a piece of writing in which you consider the issue fully, after you have discussed them all.

1 Are there situations in which you enjoy using a dialect? Explain what these are and why you enjoy them.

2 Is there anything you have read which uses dialect in an interesting way? Tell your group about it.

3 Do you use a different dialect at home from the one you use at school? What is it? Why, if you change dialects, do you do so?

4 Do you use a different dialect with your friends from the one you use in other situations? What is the dialect and why do you use it?

5 Is there any reason for studying standard English?

6 What dialects are spoken in your group? List some dialect words and expressions.

● Finally, write a story or a play in which you use a dialect. It may be your own or someone else's. You may use the dialect of standard English in your writing as long as the dialogue – the words people say – is in another dialect.

Unit 19
The language of school

Whenever a group of people has to be together or work together for any length of time they develop a special language. That is not to say that they start talking a foreign language, rather that the words of their own language have a meaning for these people over and above the meaning that the words generally have for other people.

If someone told you to 'stick a jelly on the brute' you would understandably be puzzled. You would understand all the words but still not know what to do. If you were told that this order would be given by a film cameraman to his lighting assistant and that 'a jelly' is a gelatine filter to tone down or change the colour of a light and 'the brute' is the huge light used to illuminate a film set, you might be able to begin to understand.

In the same way Cockney rhyming slang developed among people who lived and worked in the East End of London. One Cockney might say to another, 'She ain't 'arf got knobbly biscuits'. You cannot understand this until you know that 'biscuits and cheese' is rhyming slang for knees.

There are many words and phrases that have a special meaning in school that they do not have outside school. Can you think of any? Here are some.

A report
This is not what a journalist on a paper produces. It means something very precise – a piece of paper sent home to your parents about once a term on which your teachers have made notes about your progress.

A form
This is not a piece of paper you fill in to get a driving licence. In schools it means a group of pupils of roughly the same age who have their own classroom and teacher and meet twice daily for the register.

Register
The book in which attendance is recorded, to be filled in.

These are probably all words with which you are familiar, but there are many new words which 'belong' particularly to secondary school which you might not know or which you might have to explain to someone out of school.

● Can you make a list of such words? Discuss with your groups the special 'school' words which might be difficult for an outsider to understand.

Different schools have different words – it all depends on how the school is organised. You might have year heads or heads of house or form tutors or form teachers. Some words that may cause problems are:

set assembly
topic registration
theme detention

I am sure you will have many more to add to the list.

● When you have got your list try to work out a definition for your words. How would you explain them to an outsider? Write down what you would say.

Don't lose your lists and definitions. You will need them later when we look at planning a pamphlet for next year's first year in the unit called 'Using paragraphs to plan writing'.

Add your words to your dictionary.

Both you and your parents have to learn the language of school. Think about school reports; they are often written in their own kind of language. Look at this comment:

'Earl is generally a conscientious worker but he must persevere in his attempts to punctuate correctly.'

and this one:

'While Leona participates in class work with enthusiasm, I could wish she were less dilatory in handing in her homework.'

and this one:

'Greater application is called for if Simon is to improve the standard of his work.'

● In your groups, or individually, find a way of simplifying what the teachers said. You can use a dictionary if necessary.

● Now write a report on yourself. Divide your page up into sections like a real report. Try to be honest. Indicate your strengths and weaknesses and try to give yourself advice as to how to improve. Remember it is not all that helpful just to say 'Could do better' or, 'Must work harder'. Try to work out for yourself exactly what it is you could improve in and how you might do it. When you have finished your report show it to your group and ask them for their comments. Did they think you were really honest?

Do you understand how your school is run? Some schools have a pattern similar to the following:

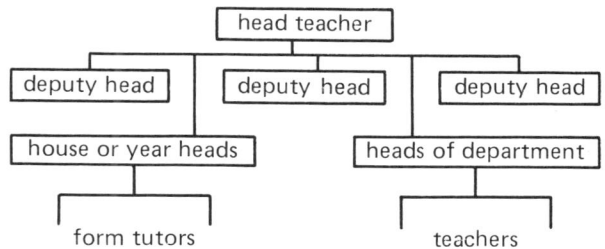

● Can you work out a diagram like this to show how your school is run? You could easily find out. Perhaps each group could send representatives to interview members of staff to find out how their jobs fit into a pattern. It might be best to start with the head teacher or one of the deputy heads because they could help you decide who else you need to see.

You would need to prepare questions in advance. What questions would you need to ask? Prepare your list in your groups and check with other groups and your teacher to make sure you have thought of all the questions you would need.

When you have finished your interviews you will probably be surprised at how much else your teachers have to do as well as teach you.

You will be able to put all your information together and make a big diagram showing how the school runs. In your diagram you can fill in names as well as titles like head of department. You could also add some brief notes as to what each job involves.

Other classes might be interested in seeing this 'who's who' in your school.

You could include it in the pamphlet for next year's first year that we are going to try to write in unit 28.

Unit 20
Words need words

Have you noticed that you can often make sense of words you have never seen before simply by reading on or looking back at what you have read? Often the words which surround new or difficult words can help you to make an intelligent guess at the meaning.

Here is a poem by Lewis Carroll. He has invented many new words but you will find that you can work out what many of them mean.

● Read the poem aloud in your groups and then discuss what the following words could mean:

frumious
vorpal
manxome
galumphing
frabjous

When you have come to some agreement, try to explain to your group or to other groups exactly how you worked out the meaning.

Jabberwocky

'Twas brillig, and the slithy toves
Did gyre and gimble in the wabe,
All mimsy were the borogoves,
And the mome raths outgrabe.

"Beware the Jabberwock, my son!
The jaws that bite, the claws that catch!
Beware the Jubjub bird and shun
The frumious Bandersnatch!"

He took his vorpal sword in hand:
Long time the manxome foe he sought
So rested he by the Tumtum tree
And stood awhile in thought.

And as in uffish thought he stood,
The Jabberwock, with eyes of flame,
Came whiffling through the tulgey wood,
And burbled as it came!

One, two! One, two! And through and through
The vorpal blade went snicker-snack!
He left it dead, and with its head
He went galumphing back.

"And hast thou slain the Jabberwock?
Come to my arms my beamish boy!
O frabjous day! Callooh! Callay!
He chortled in his joy.

'Twas brillig, and the slithy toves
Did gyre and gimble in the wabe;
All mimsy were the borogoves,
And the mome raths outgrabe.

Lewis Carroll

Alice asked Humpty Dumpty to explain the first verse of this poem in *Alice Through the Looking Glass*. Here's his version. What do you think of it?

'You seem very clever at explaining words, Sir,' said Alice. 'Would you kindly tell me the meaning of the poem called "Jabberwocky"?'
'Let's hear it,' said Humpty Dumpty. 'I can explain all the poems that ever were invented—and a good many that haven't been invented just yet.'
This sounded very hopeful, so Alice repeated the first verse:

*'Twas brillig, and the slithy toves
 Did gyre and gimble in the wabe:
All mimsy were the borogoves,
 And the mome raths outgrabe.'*

'That's enough to begin with,' Humpty Dumpty interrupted: 'there are plenty of hard words there. *"Brillig"* means four o'clock in the afternoon—the time when you begin *broiling* things for dinner.'
'That'll do very well,' said Alice: 'and *"slithy"*?'
'Well, *"slithy"* means "lithe and slimy".'

"Lithe" is the same as "active". You see it's like a portmanteau—there are two meanings packed up into one word.'

'I see it now,' Alice remarked thoughtfully: 'and what are "toves"?'

'Well, "toves" are something like badgers—they're something like lizards—and they're something like corkscrews.'

'They must be very curious-looking creatures.'

'They are that,' said Humpty Dumpty: 'also they make their nests under sundials—also they live on cheese.'

'And what's to "gyre" and to "gimble"?'

'To "gyre" is to go round and round like a gyroscope. To "gimble" is to make holes like a gimlet.'

'And "the wabe," is the grass-plot round a sundial, I suppose?' said Alice, surprised at her own ingenuity.

'Of course it is. It's called "wabe," you know, because it goes a long way before it, and a long way behind it—'

'And a long way beyond it on each side,' Alice added.

'Exactly so. Well then "mimsy" is "flimsy and miserable" (there's another portmanteau for you). And a "borogove" is a thin shabby-looking bird with its feathers sticking out all round—something like a live mop.'

'And then "mome raths"?' said Alice. 'I'm afraid I'm giving you a great deal of trouble.'

'Well, a "rath" is a sort of green pig: but "mome" I'm not certain about. I think it's short for "from home"—meaning that they'd lost their way, you know.'

'And what does "outgrabe" mean?'

'Well, "outgribing" is something between bellowing and whistling, with a kind of sneeze in the middle: however, you'll hear it done, maybe—down in the wood yonder—and when you've once heard it you'll be *quite* content. Who's been repeating all that hard stuff to you?'

Unit 21
Using context clues

The sentence or passage in which a word appears can help you get a good idea of what it might mean. The *context* provides a *clue*. This is how you were able to make some interesting guesses about the nonsense words in the 'Jabberwocky'. All of us come across words we don't know when we are reading or listening to someone talk, but we don't have to keep stopping to check in a dictionary to find out what they mean. We make guesses. We pick up clues.

It helps us understand this process and get better at making guesses if we know something more about the kind of clues we are given.

● Here are some examples of difficult words and clues that might help you understand them. In your groups, or individually, try to:
(a) explain the words which are printed in *italics*
(b) explain what the clues to their meanings are, and how they helped you.
Here are your words and their contexts:

1 My brother *scoffed*, not with words but with snorts through the nose, at the idea of any girl being brave.

2 Then fear and relief both gave way to a great aggressive *loathing* for that swine Smith for telling on him.

3 It (the hut) was low and dusky, windowless, fragrant with herbs that hung drying from the cross pole of the roof, mint and *moly* and thyme, *yarrow* and *rushwash* and *paramal*, *kingsfoil*, *clovenfoot*, *tansy* and bay.

4 Keith breathed a temporary sigh of relief. Trouble had been *averted*, and he was pleased about that, but he knew very well this couldn't go on for ever.

5 The students need to understand the teacher's requirements and *standards* of *assessment* – what makes it good or bad in the teacher's judgement.

6 The children and their parents were too *flabbergasted* to speak. They were staggered. They were *dumbfounded*. They were bewildered and dazzled. They were completely bowled over with the hugeness of the thing.

7 Earlier there had been rain and certain roots and growths had caught a *phosphorescence*; spots of light glimmered in the bushy nothingness.

8 Besides, I'd never let on to my husband, but the summer trips are *tedious*, just back and forth up and down the river.

How many of the words could you understand? You might not have got the complete meaning, but you probably were able to make an intelligent guess so that you could follow the overall meaning. What kind of clues did you find? Here are some that you might have used.

1 *Using your own experience.* This would help with numbers one and two.
(a) Some boys think girls are not as brave as they. You can imagine how a boy might react to the idea of a girl being brave. So you can guess what 'scoffed' means.
(b) What do pupils feel about someone who 'tells on' them? You know about that, so you can guess what 'loathing' might mean.

2 *Words in a list* give clues for number three. You are told that there are herbs hanging from the roof of the hut. There is a long list which includes the names of some herbs you might already know. What are the other strange things likely to be?

3 Sometimes a *comparison* or *contrast* gives a clue. This helps with number four. Keith knows his relief can't go on for ever. There is trouble around. So we can guess what 'trouble had been averted' might mean. It certainly hasn't gone away for good.

4 Sometimes a writer *sums up* a word or phrase for us. This clue helps with number five: 'What makes it good or bad in the teacher's judgement' helps us guess what 'standards of assessment' means.

5 The *mood* of a passage can give us a clue to the hard words in number six. The parents

and children are bewildered and dazzled. Perhaps that clue helps us guess what 'flabbergasted' and 'dumbfounded' mean.

6 Sometimes a difficult word is simply *explained* for us. Can you see how this happens in numbers seven and eight?

● Now something to do in your groups. Imagine you are a writer and you are using some difficult words. Write sentences in which you use a context clue to help your reader understand the meaning. You can either make up these words, for example:

Susan's glee on seeing the parcel turned to total *glumphishness* when she realised it was not for her,

or you can look up new words in the dictionary.
Try out your context clues on your group and see if your friends can guess the meaning of the words.

Some guidelines

When not to use a dictionary

1 If you are given a direct explanation.

2 If the clues give you a great deal of help and the meaning you have guessed fits in with the rest of the passage.

3 If you only need a general sense of the meaning.

When to use a dictionary

1 If you need a precise meaning of the word.

2 If the clues suggest several possibilities and you cannot decide which is correct.

3 If you cannot understand nearby words.

4 If you meet the word frequently and know it will be useful to you, a precise meaning is therefore needed.

Unit 22
How do we read?

We saw in the last unit that reading involves guessing. It's just like listening, really. When you read or hear a new word, you pick up clues from the context, the words around it, and they help you guess the meaning. But that isn't the only kind of guess we make when we read. We often guess what's coming next. We do that in listening too.

Look at this transcript. Three girls are discussing the film *Gale Is Dead*. The film has shown how Gale, an unwanted child, eventually became a drug addict. The girls were very sorry for Gale and thought that her real problem was that she couldn't trust anyone.

If you read the transcript aloud in your groups you can see how the listeners *guessed* what was going to be said next.

Juliet: Over the years/it takes a period of time/she loved her mother for so many years/and she tried to make her mother appreciate her/and she appreciated her mother as well/but after a while/I think someone can take so much of/you know/being hated/that she hated her mother in the end so much because she didn't/you know/her mother just didn't care about her.

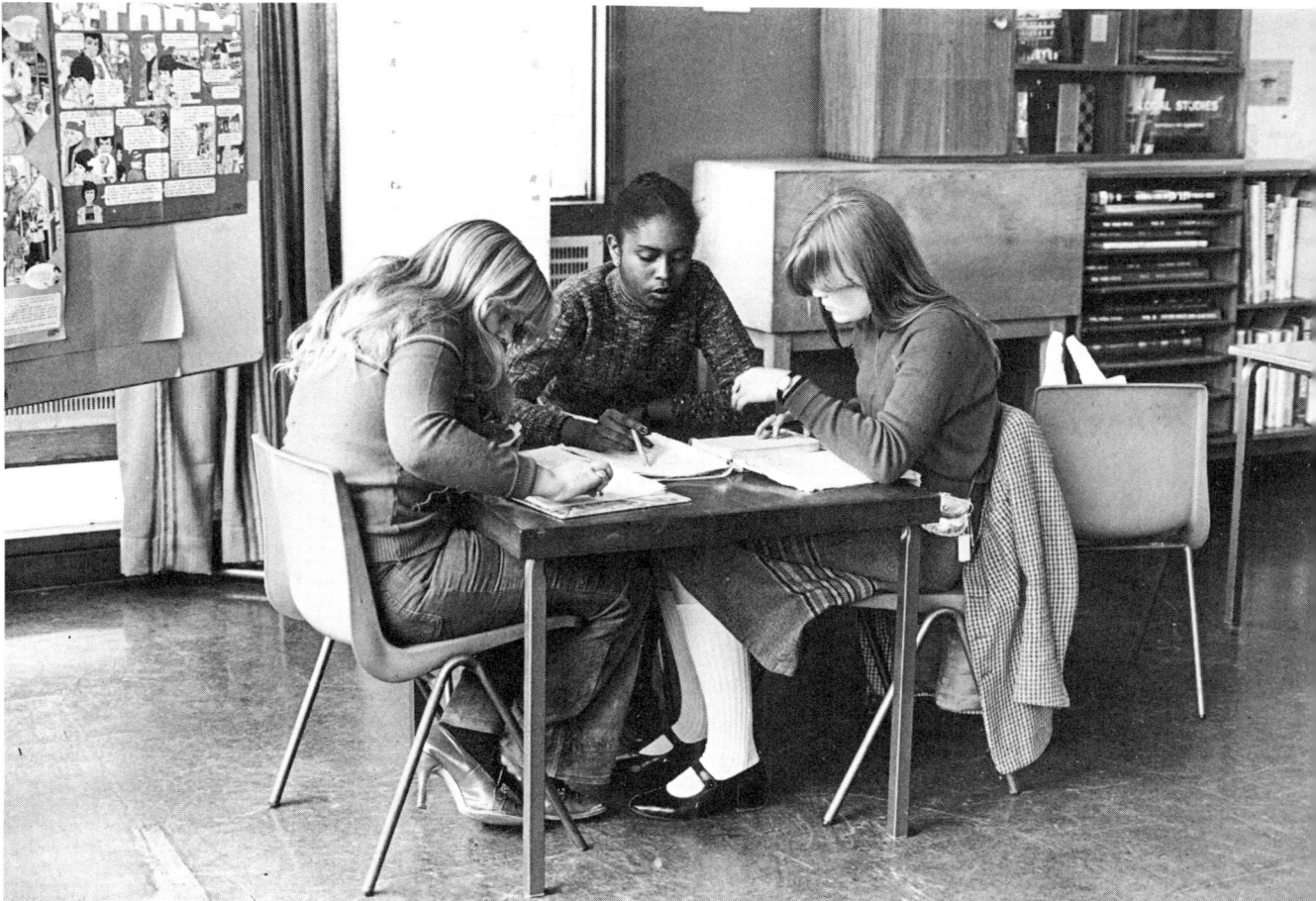

Sandra: I mean/she was only young then really/and she loved being with her mum/but when she probably got older/and found out like/what really happened/you know . . .

Katy: She understood that strangers loved her/I mean that woman . . .

Juliet: Mrs David

Sandra: Mrs David/right

Katy: She had more love for her than her mother/but she didn't really really want to hang on it/you know.

Did you notice how Katy completed a sentence for Sandra, and that both Juliet and Sandra knew that when Katy said 'that woman' she meant Mrs David?

If you read the transcript again only silently this time, you can see that the whole thing could almost have been said by one person. Because the girls have all seen the same film and felt the same sympathy for Gale, one of them can easily guess where another is leading them in the discussion and join in.

How is this like reading? Look at this extract. This is a cloze passage, that means several words have been missed out. Read it quickly to yourself. What is it about?

My name . . . Timothy Mackart. I was . . . and grew . . . in Jamaica. It was . . . the country. My . . . had a farm, where . . . grew tobacco, peas . . . beans. It wasn't a . . . big farm, but it . . . enough . . . keep . . . busy . . . bring in . . . the cash. What . . . liked most . . . the farm was how . . . . . . distance . . . plants seemed . . . have evenly grown, but . . . I came . . . close it . . . completely different.

You could follow the passage easily because you either:

1 knew what was coming next – like the listeners and talkers in the transcript or

2 could read on and guess the missing word with the help of the next words.

So you don't need to read every individual word to follow a passage.

You read   groups of words   at a time and your eye moves backwards and forwards along the line stopping in the middle of each group.

This dot   shows where   your eye might be as it moves   along the line

Try
reading
this
sentence
and
you
will
see
how
strange
it
feels
to
read
words
one
by
one

So you know some things about reading. You know:

1 That you pick up clues about meaning from the whole passage.

2 That you guess what's coming next quite often and therefore don't need to read every word.

3 That you also read words in groups, not individually.

● Try out your reading skills in groups on this cloze passage. Make an intelligent guess as to what are the missing words. Sometimes you'll guess what's coming next, sometimes you'll

have to read on to get the clues. In many cases there are several words which might fit the gap. Choose the one you think fits best.

As far as the eye can see, scarlet . . . . . are marching. The hillside is in bloom with them. Regiment upon . . . . . . are mounting as if to capture the sun. There is a sound of drumming in the air that alarms the . . . . . . so that they wheel and flutter higher and higher till they are no more than black . . . . . . on the complexion of the sky.

They have risen from a . . . . . . that crowns the western side of the hilltop. It is not very large, this wood, but singularly dark; and under the sun it casts a sharp black . . . . . . before it – like a pit.

Now comes a . . . . . . that flutters the advancing pennants and briskens the glinting lines. They are like a tide – a . . . . . . of scarlet waves, flecked with silver, brass, white and blue. A rich and splendid company; and none more so than the drummer boy.

He marches there, raising his . . . . . . almost haughtily as he thunders out the Advance. His eyes are bright and he smiles triumphantly as tall men grin and nod and secretly wave: for he is well-liked . . . being young, sturdy and full of hope.

Perhaps he struts a little, but no one minds. The drummer boy is their golden . . . . . . and he's caught the rhythm of their hearts.

It is to this . . . . . . that they march, and the drummer . . . . . . has the strange feeling that the shining regiments, rising and falling with a regular rustling thump as their black boots tread the grass, are the obedient spirits of his drum.

It is the grandest . . . . . . of his brief life. He glances up, as if to challenge the heavens to show anything finer than the glory mounting the hillside.

69

● When your group has decided on its list of words, compare them with the words other groups chose and discuss which words fit best and why.

If you want to check with the original, you should find Leon Garfield's novel *The Drummer Boy*. This is the opening section.

● Can you prepare another cloze passage for another class to use? How do you prepare a cloze passage? Look at the extract below.

1 Read the extract through in your groups.

2 Now look at it carefully section by section. Which words can be taken out? Remember other pupils need all the clues that you have been using to fill the gaps.

3 Try to choose carefully the words you will take out so that other pupils will see that reading involves
(a) guessing what comes next
(b) reading on to make more sense of what has just been read.

4 Try to take out some words that will make another group of pupils really discuss a number of different words which might fit the gap. You will need to explain to them that they will have to make choices between a number of words and they should choose the one that fits best. Decide what you will write as an introduction to the passage.

5 When you have finished discussing what words you should leave out, write some instructions to the other class explaining:
(a) what you mean them to learn by looking at the passage and discussing what words should fit the gaps
(b) how they should set about it.

6 Compare your instructions and the words you have omitted with those of other groups.

7 Decide a final version with the whole class.

8 If it's possible some of you might visit the class that is using your cloze passage and report back to your own class as to how they coped with it.

Here is the extract. It is taken from a book called *Small Accidents* by Sabir Bandali. The book tells the story of his life from his childhood in Uganda to his present life as a student in London. In this extract he is remembering his first day at school.

The school uniform consisted of a pair of black shorts, a white short-sleeved shirt, white socks and black shoes. It took me only a few minutes to get dressed, so that when my mother came to wake me up at 6.45, I was already prepared to go to school. She was astonished, but very proud of me.

At last it was time to leave. Mina and I were to go to school with our domestic servant, Agusto. School wasn't very far away, but Agusto found me too slow and carried me the remaining distance to school as if I was a new-born baby. I didn't mind because I didn't have to worry about where I was stepping and had more time to think about where I was going. My sister was fussy about where I put my feet because she knew I had a tendency to fall at every step. I knew that my mind was on more important things than my feet.

Once I had entered the school, I was led back outside! The rain had now stopped but we had to listen to a speech by the headmaster which was tedious and hard to understand. This was another time in my life when I felt confused. I wasn't used to crowds, for as a small boy I hadn't gone out much, but used to play near home. I began to feel so dizzy that my sister, who was now blushing, had to come and hold me up. The other pupils were laughing and I started blushing because I was angry. I thought they were stupid and inconsiderate.

Since it was January, the beginning of a new year in school, the chairs were on the tables. The teacher told us to sit anywhere on any chair. I was still a little confused and without thinking I climbed onto the table and onto the chair sitting on top. I sat down too confidently. The pupils and the teacher started to laugh loudly. I got more confused and not realising the joke, I too started laughing. My style of laughing was so unique (tears roll out of my eyes when I actually laugh even to this day) that I fell off the chair. It was then that I noticed that everybody else had taken their chairs off the table and were sitting on them.

At the end of school at 4 o'clock, Mina and I went towards home. She knew the way and anyway, she had already made a few friends so getting home was easier. All the way home I was ignored for my stupidity shown in the various incidents of this day. Now I felt lonely. In actual fact I felt so lonely and dejected that I ran away from the bunch and made towards what I thought was home. I passed a few shops but none of them looked familiar so I kept walking at a slower pace, looking around as if I was window-shopping, to disguise the fact that I was lost. At length I came to a clearing. I recognised this because it was the only place I knew – I had often gone out there because it was next to our home. I ecstatically ran into the shop where I was met by my father.

'What did you learn at School, Sabir?'

'Oh, many things,' I answered thoughtfully.

'Like what for example?' I hesitated, so he made it simpler. 'What is one plus one?'

'Oh, we haven't got that far yet,' I answered, quite satisfied with myself. My father looked at me and smiled.

Unit 23
Reading in different ways

Reading involves making guesses. One of the reasons that we read groups of words together is that we make good guesses about what groups of words go together.

Really good readers can alter the way they read. Sometimes they read very quickly, other times very slowly. Sometimes a reader needs to glance over a page to see if it contains anything of interest, at other times it's necessary to read carefully and in detail.

Reading quickly

It is very useful to be able to do this. You *can* increase your reading speed. There are several ways of doing this.

Making good guesses
If you concentrate on what you are reading you will pick up more clues and therefore be able to guess at what is coming next.

If you already have some idea what is coming next, your guesses will be better. You can often glance down a page and pick out a few phrases that will prepare you for what's coming up.

Paragraphs are a great help here. Each one has its own particular topic as you can see in a later unit, 'Looking at paragraphs'. So you can look quickly at each paragraph to see what it is about and then start to read the page. This process of glancing at the whole page, picking out the main points, is called *skimming*.

Beat the clock
You can actually train yourself to read faster just as you can train to run faster. Time your reading. How many pages can you read in five minutes? Can you beat your record? Remember the important thing is that you should understand what you are reading. There's no point in racing so fast that you don't see anything on the way. With practice you will speed up.

Decide why you are reading

If you just want the general gist of a passage, then you can read quickly and skim over the page. On the other hand, if you want to follow a complicated plot or enjoy a poem or read something difficult you will need to read slowly and carefully.

Reading carefully

Unless you are reading a novel where you don't want to know what happens next, a quick skim of the whole passage will help you read more carefully, because you will have some idea of where the writer is taking you to, what points are going to be raised next.

Again the paragraphs are useful, because each one has its own topic. You should ask yourself what each one is about as you read it. You have skimmed and got an overall picture, now you look at the passage bit by bit and see how each bit of the jigsaw fits together.

● Try reading this passage.

1 *Skim* over it, looking for the main ideas using the paragraphs as a guide.

2 *Read it through carefully* seeing how each paragraph fits in.

The Discovery of the New World
The first European sailors to set foot on the vast continent of America were probably the Vikings of Denmark and Norway. Their longships made their way across the North Atlantic by way of Iceland and Greenland and visited America during the eleventh century A.D. Nearly five hundred years were to pass before European sailors again travelled across the Atlantic.

The great discoverers of the fifteenth century did not sail simply out of curiosity. A desire for wealth and riches was one of their strongest motives. Europe wanted spices, clothes, and jewels from the East and people were prepared to pay high prices for them. These goods were first brought to Europe along the overland route through Constantinople. When that city was captured by the Turks in 1453, new routes to

the East had to be found. The Portuguese discovered a way to India by sailing round the southern tip of Africa; but, as many European seamen were now convinced that the earth was round, they believed that India could be reached by sailing westwards.

In 1492, Christopher Columbus, a Genoese seaman in the pay of Spain, set out westwards on such a voyage. After sailing for thirty-three days with so sign of land, his discontented crew were demanding to turn back when they sighted a vast new continent. Another Italian explorer who had come to Spain, Amerigo Vespucci, gave his name to this New World; he probably first sailed to America in 1497.

In the same year (1497), John and Sebastian Cabot reached Newfoundland from the English port of Bristol. Their voyage did not produce a rich harvest of treasure but it gave England an important claim when settlers began to colonise the new continent.

The French also took part in exploring America. Jacques Cartier worked his way down the St. Lawrence river (1535), as did Samuel Champlain, another great Frenchman (1608). Later La Salle travelled from the St. Lawrence to the Gulf of Mexico (1682). Their journeys helped to open up territory which today forms part of the United States.

The great English sailors of the time of Queen Elizabeth I—Raleigh, Gilbert and Drake—also discovered a great deal of information about the coastline of North America. Their own attempts to start colonies failed but they set an example which was to be eagerly followed during the next century.

Scanning

Sometimes you don't need to read a whole book or a chapter if you are simply trying to find one or two pieces of information.

If you are trying to find information from a non-fiction book then you should first turn to the *index*. This is a kind of tin-opener. It helps you get into the book.

The index will tell you what page or pages the information you want will be on. If there is no index then you have to use the contents list at the beginning of the book. We will look at how to use an index in the next unit.

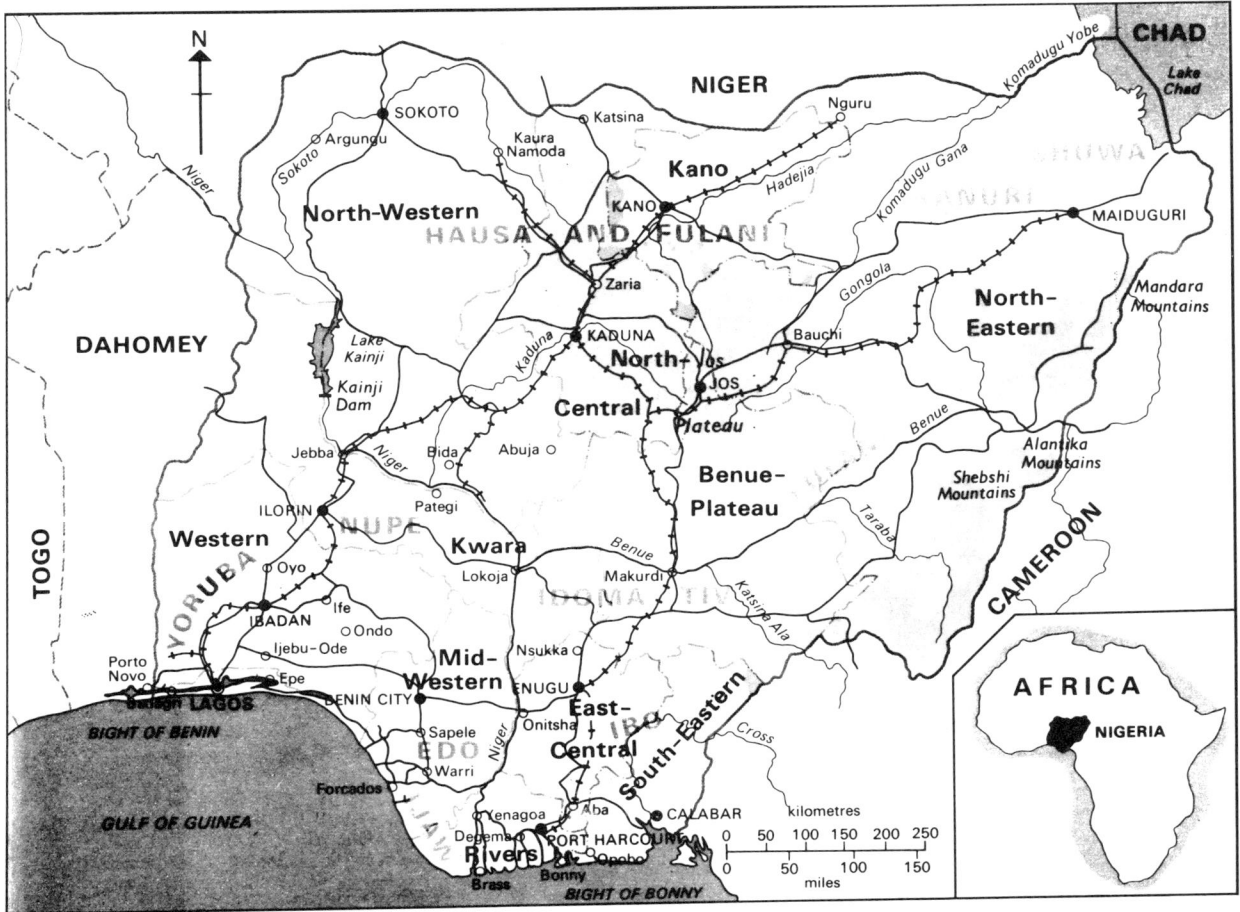

A map of Nigeria showing states, cities, tribes, rivers, railways and boundaries, with an inset map of Africa.

International boundaries ······ Main roads ——— Federal capital ⊙
Nigerian boundary ——— NUPE Tribes ——— Densely populated areas
State boundaries ········ State capitals ● Land over 2000 feet (609 metres)
Railways +++++

Once you have found your page you *scan* it for the facts you want. It's rather like finding a place on a map.

● Look at this map of Nigeria and try to find Nsukka and Oyo. When you look for these places, you have an image in your mind of the length of the word and its shape and you glance over the whole map looking for words which fit that pattern. You only really read likely-looking words.

You do the same thing when you *scan* a page of print. You have an idea about the thing you are looking for and you glance down the page until you see something that looks as if it might fit. Only then do you stop and actually read.

● Try scanning this passage to find the following pieces of information.

Which part of America did Catholics settle in?
When was Georgia founded?
Where was the first English settlement in America?

Remember: don't read the whole passage, just spot the sections you need.

The Thirteen Colonies

The continent of America provided a wonderful opportunity for Europeans to escape from troubles at home. English, French, Dutch and Swedes flocked to North America.

The French usually settled in the region around the St. Lawrence river. The Dutch went much further south to found their colony of New Amsterdam, known later as New York after its capture by the English in 1664. New Sweden grew up around the mouth of the Delaware River, but it, too, was taken over by the English, for most settlers in the seventeenth century came from England.

In 1607, the first permanent English settlement in what was later to be the United States was founded in Virginia at the mouth of the James River. Despite the dangers arising from famine, disease and Indians, the new colony grew steadily, especially when a method of tobacco curing was introduced.

In 1620, another group of English people sailed to join them in the now famous *Mayflower*. Bad weather forced the little ship northwards and instead of reaching Virginia, the Mayflower party laid the foundations of the New England colonies. These colonies—Massachusetts, Rhode Island, New Hampshire and Connecticut—grew steadily. To the south, the colonies of Maryland and North and South Carolina helped to complete a chain of British colonies down the east coast of North America. The number reached thirteen with the foundation of Georgia in 1732.

People went to America because its great size offered them *freedom*. Sometimes it was religious freedom, sometimes freedom from the fear of unemployment, and sometimes freedom from tyranny. All these reasons played a part in the founding of the British colonies. The New England settlers were mostly Puritans escaping from religious persecution at home.

Pennsylvania takes its name from William Penn, leader of the Quakers, who were also persecuted in England. Charles II granted Penn the ownership of the colony. Catholics found refuge in Maryland; Church of England followers persecuted in turn by the Puritans went to Virginia.

On the other hand, Georgia was set up first as an attempt to find homes for debtors. Virginia and South Carolina attracted people who had lost land and employment in England. The seventeenth century saw thousands of Englishmen who were out of work turn to America for an answer to their problem.

There was, in fact, enough room in the thirteen colonies for any one to make a fresh start and to escape from harsh laws at home. For those people brave enough to face the hazardous Atlantic crossing, a new land of opportunity beckoned.

Unit 24
Using an index

Indexes are vital because they help you find your way around a book. They save you time – you can find what you need quickly and you can decide easily whether a book contains what you want.

Opposite is an index from a book on China.

How does it work?

1 Everything is in alphabetical order just like a dictionary.

2 Some entries give you only one page reference – look at **abacus**. That is only mentioned on one page.

3 Other entries have several page references – look at **Mongolia**. There is information about that on five pages. You would have to scan each page to see if the information there was any use to you.

4 People are indexed in alphabetical order according to their surname rather than their first name, so Marco Polo the explorer can be found under **Polo, Marco** as you can see from the index. So you always look up people by their surname: Shakespeare, William; Dickens, Charles etc.

5 Do you notice there are no 'the's'? The Soviet Union is indexed as **Soviet Union**, the Great Wall is indexed as **Great Wall**. That is because we put 'the' in front of many words and phrases and the list of 'the's' would be very long. The index concentrates on the main word or words.

6 You have to be quite clear about what you are looking for in an index and be prepared to think 'how else could my topic be indexed?' For example, if you wanted to know about rivers in China you would find nothing under '**rivers**' in the index, but look at '**waterways**' and there's four pages for you.

● Can you find your way round this index? Discuss the following questions in your groups.

1 If you wanted to find out about how Chinese people dress what page should you turn to?

2 Where would you find out about the ways they speak?

3 What page would you look at to find what games they play?

4 Where would you find information about Chinese schools?

Index

Unit 25
Proof-reading your work

When we looked at reading we saw that good readers make guesses, they expect certain words to come up and therefore don't really read each word. Sometimes when you read your own work, you do the same thing and therefore leave lots of mistakes in simply because, being a good reader, you did not see them.

Look at this story and discuss it in your groups.

The Best Composition of All Time
He glanced sideways as he heard the rapid scratch of Charlie's pen beside him. He was able to make out the top line of Charlie's composition. 'When the manks cam they fun Heerward unconcon.' He felt gingerly about with his clog-toe for Charlie's foot.

'Get off me flappin' toe – can't you?' said Charlie.

He took his foot away at once and the violent scratching of Charlie's pen went on. If she sees it she'll clout him and he's that near that I feel it.

'Who the 'eck art nudgin'?' asked Charlie loudly.

He bent his head, listened, waiting for Miss Skegham to go out. At last the door closed behind her. The buzz of talk began. He turned to Charlie.

'Stop!' he said. 'What's that?'

'What's what?'

'When the manks cam they fun Heerward unconcon.'

'What art talkin' about, M'Cloud? There are times when I think tha must be goin' off they nut.'

'Read that top line of thine, Crid. Just read it.'

'I can see nowt wrong with it.'

'What's a mank?'

'Mank? Mank? Oh, tha means monk!'

'Then why not write monk, Chey?'

'Oh – flappin' Nora! Thanks, Mike.'

'Who's Heerward, Chey?'

'What the 'ell art talkin' about?'

'I said who's Heerward?'

'Heerward? Oh, Hereward – you piecan.'

'Then put Hereward – if it's Hereward the Wake, Chey. What's fun?'

'"Fun"? "Fun's" fun. I fun a penny in the street.'

'Tha'll fun four raps with her stick if tha doesn't change it. Found, you daft nut.'

'Oh holy mackerel, so it is, Mike. Quick is there owt else?'

'Put an "e" on came. Chey, what's "unconcon"?'

'I'm blowed if I know what tha'rt talkin about!'

'Tha'll be blowed if tha doesn't. Should it be "unconscious"?'

'Holy Moses, I were goin' at it that fast I didn't have time to cudgitate. Go over it, Mike.'

'That sounds a bit odd to me, Chey – "He had thick golden hair growing down the back of his chest."'

'What's odd about it?'

'Holy Mother, that would mean down his lungs, wouldn't it? He couldn't have hair growing down his lungs, could he?'

'He could, perhaps – but it's not likely tha'd have heard about it, Chey.'

'An' me thinkin' I'd written the best composition of all time,' said Charley, 'that 'ud have been framed in letters of gold in the school hall, whereas I'd ha' got my bum smacked. Comes from not cudgitatin', Mike. I'll remember thee in my will.'

The door-latch clicked and the class went silent as Miss Skegham entered. He went on with his own composition.

●

1 How many of Charlie's mistakes had you spotted?

2 Why do you think he made them?

3 Why was he unable to spot his mistakes even when Mike first pointed them out to him?

4 Have you ever gone over your work with someone other than a teacher? If so, did you find it useful? If you haven't done so, do you think you would find it useful to try?

This process of re-reading your work to look for errors is called *proof-reading*. You can do it by yourself or with a friend. How does it work?

Proof-reading your own work

By working with other people you learn to spot the difference between what you meant to write and what you have actually written. Although it is useful to have someone else point this out to you, it is not always possible. There are one or two points to bear in mind here.

You should leave a time gap between your writing and your re-reading. If you try to proof-read immediately you have finished writing, you will be in danger of reading what you meant to write.

When you re-read, try to pretend that you are someone else and ask yourself if the piece of writing actually makes sense to someone else and how it could be improved.

With a friend

We have seen an example of this in the story we have read. It is useful to have someone else read what you have written. When you write something it may make complete sense to you at the time, like Charlie writing that Hereward 'had thick golden hair growing down the back of his chest'. Because it made sense to you at the time, when you re-read the passage it may still make sense to you.

Spelling errors are often just the same. When you read what you have written you often assume that you have spelled the words the way they should be spelled. Charlie looked at 'mank' and read 'monk'. It took Mike to point out that it was wrong and as soon as he pointed out that Charlie had written 'mank', then he was able to correct it. He knew all along how to spell the word, but had not noticed that he had got it wrong.

The same is true of punctuation. When you write 'Mary Ellen made the cakes.' You might mean just that or you might mean 'Mary, Ellen made the cakes'. A second reader will be able to point out to you what you have written, not what you meant to write.

It is very valuable for you to proof-read other people's work because you will quickly learn what kinds of mistakes can be made by not thinking hard about what you are writing. You learn from your own mistakes and also from other people's! This helps you to proof-read by yourself.

Do not be afraid to rewrite

Very few people can always write down what they want to say, in the way they want to say it, at the first attempt. Very often you will need to have a first attempt at writing something. This piece of writing is called the first draft, and then, when you have re-read it, you will scribble in extra bits, cross out sections, maybe even tear the whole thing up and start again. Most really good writers go through first, second, third and even fourth and more drafts before they are satisfied with what they have written. Even poets work like this. John Keats used to work all day writing and rewriting something until he got it right. Some days he would produce nothing, other days he would have four lines of poetry and others he might have written much more.

Some of you will have read the adventures of Nigel Molesworth, and his younger brother Molesworth 2 in *How to be Topp* by Geoffrey Williams and Ronald Searle. Certainly Molesworth does not think much of school and spends his English lessons throwing pellets at his class mates.

In this section of the book, Molesworth is discussing the delights that await new boys on their first day at 'St Custards'.

● Can you proof-read his work and rewrite it correctly?

How to succeed as a new bug

New bugs are wets and weeds their mummies blub when they kiss them goodbye while seniors such as me hemhem stand grimly by licking their slobering chops. No more dolies or William the bear to cuddle and hug, no more fairy stories at nany's knee it is all aboard the fairy bus for the dungeons. You hav to hav a bit of patience but once the trane moves out the little victims are YOURS. You put them in the lugage rack with molesworth 2.

Paters* at the moment are patting the blubing maters.*

'It is all right, old girl,' they sa. 'Skools are not wot they were in my day. Boys are no longer cruel to each other and the masters are frends.'

'But my Eustace hav been taken away. He is only a baby.'

(You are dead right he is. Fancy sending him to skool with a name like Eustace. They deserve it all.)

Pater stare at his glass of gin reflectively. It will be peaceful at home now. He can relax at the weekends and if it is good skool Eustace will soon be strong and brany enuff to bring in the coal. He sa:

'Now in my day it was diferent. When i first went to Grunts they tosted me on a slo fire. Then i ran the gauntlet being flicked with wet towels. Then they stood me aganst the mantelpeace as i am standing now –'
BANG! CRASH!
Mater give him sharp uper cut folowed by right cross then zoom up to bed leaving pater wondering why women are so unpredictable. Glumly he pours himself another gin.

* Pater and Mater are the Latin words for father and mother.

When you are proof-reading a friend's work you could use some signs to show what kind of mistakes have been made.

People who check through books before they are printed use many such signs. They are called proof-correction marks. It works like this. A sign is put in the margin – called a marginal mark – and the error is marked in the actual writing.

Here is an example. If someone has missed a capital letter you would write 'caps' in the margin and draw a circle round the letter which should be altered.

Here are some more set out in a table.

Marginal mark	Meaning	Mark in the writing
n.p.	new paragraph needed	[before first word of new paragraph
run on ∧	no fresh paragraph needed	～ between paragraphs
	something is missed out. You show in the margin what it is so a missing full stop would be ∧ .	∧ where something should be put in
sp	word wrongly spelt	underline word
" "	quotation marks needed	∧ ∧
lc	change from capitals to lower case (small letters)	draw a circle round letters to be altered

There are other signs you could also use like:
? = doesn't make sense
X = wrong
√ = good point
The important thing is that you agree what signs you will use and stick to them.

Unit 26
Paragraphs are sense units

● Look at this example of paragraphing from a book on Chinese cookery. In your groups discuss what the topic of each paragraph is.

Everything you read is in sense units.

A book is a sense unit. It is all about one topic or linked topics. Even encyclopedias are in sense units. Each volume is about topics whose titles come under a range of letters of the alphabet A – E or D – F and so on.

A chapter is a sense unit within a book. In a narrative book – one which tells a story – each chapter takes the action a bit further. In a non-fiction book each chapter discusses a different aspect of the subject under consideration.

A paragraph is a sense unit within a chapter. Each paragraph has its own topic; it may be linked to the paragraphs before it and after it, but it has its own special topic.

It is very useful to realise this because when you are reading something difficult or something you have to concentrate on, you can use the paragraphs to help you follow the argument, as you saw in the unit called 'How do we read?'

There are two ways of indicating where a new paragraph starts. The first word may start a little way in from the margin. This is called *indenting*. Sometimes a line is left between paragraphs.

Both indenting and leaving a line are visual signs to the reader. They say, 'Look out, here comes a new topic or stage in the story'. You are all familiar with the convention of leaving gaps between words; if we wrote likethisallthetime it would be difficult to sort out what we meant. The paragraph gap is just the same. It is a convention, or a generally agreed sign, which is used when we want to separate one thing from another.

Perhaps the first thing any would-be Chinese cook learns is what the Chinese consider to be the basic ingredients of cooking. We Chinese say that to begin housekeeping there are seven *must* items: oil, salt, soy sauce, vinegar, fuel, rice and tea. Let's talk about each of these items individually.

The most widely used cooking oil in China is bean oil extracted from soy beans. Others include peanut oil, cabbage-seed oil, sesame-seed oil, cotton-seed oil, lard, chicken fat, and sometimes even duck fat. For family cooking, peanut oil is the odds-on favourite because it is considered the 'best tasting' – that is, it is least likely to disturb the taste of the food prepared with it. When preparing a banquet, however, most Chinese restaurants are apt to use lard. Whenever chicken fat is used in particular dishes, most restaurants will announce the fact in their menus. Butter is rarely used; there has always been a scarcity of dairy products in China and the majority of Chinese have never acquired a taste for it.

The common, ordinary variety of table salt is taken for granted by Westerners because, well, it *is* so common and ordinary. Not so in China, where salt is often a prized commodity. The Chinese obtain most of their salt through the evaporation of sea water. For the people living in China's interior provinces, thousands of miles from the coast, salt is often hard to come by. Because of inadequate transportation facilities, it is difficult and costly to carry salt to the inland regions. In the past, the taxes levied by local authorities on each shipment as it passed through their provinces so inflated the price of salt that most families could not afford it. This was the reason that, in certain regions of China, cooks took to using vinegar and not peppers as salt substitutes to bring out flavor in food.

The one ingredient that most characterizes Chinese cookery is a dark, salty liquid that goes under the name of soy sauce. All types of soy sauce are made from soy beans, water and salt, although the sauce comes in many grades and shades of color, from dark brown to darker brown to darkest brown. Various regions of China produce their own types of soy sauce, differing according to the techniques of the makers and the source and quality of the water used (just as in brewing beer, familiar factors impart distinctive characteristics to the final product). Soy sauce of a serviceable if undistinguished type can be bought at many Continental delicatessen-type grocery shops and even at large supermarkets.

The author goes on to discuss all the other basics and concludes with:

These basic seven are the most important ingredients in Chinese cooking, but, of course, one can hardly cook a palatable meal with these alone.

The author begins by telling us what the paragraphs are to be about, deals neatly with each topic, giving each a paragraph and concludes by reminding us about what she has said before leading on to the next section, so we are guided through the article.

You will find that fiction often works in a similar way. Look at this section from *Skinny Nancy* by Bill Naughton.

We moved to Lancashire when I was a boy. I felt lost and lonely there after the silent stretches of my Irish Mayo, bog and hill, treeless and sweet-aired. So my mother slipped me extra pocket-money to ease my misery, and with this I wormed my way in among my new mates.

'If that's your own tanner,' Albert Monks said to me one Friday evening, 'I can take you to a right good shop for spending it – Skinny Nancy's.' His hand on my shoulder along the street, he said, 'You're right lucky I'm with you, because she's the tightest skinflint ever drew breath, an' she'd have that sixpence out of your pocket before you knew what was happening.'

The shop window was so grimed that we couldn't see inside until we'd breathed on the glass and polished it up with our jersey sleeves. For a moment all I saw was a blurred interior, until suddenly the contents came clearly into focus.

The first paragraph sets the scene and tells you about the money. The second paragraph shows how the boy is invited by his friend to go to Skinny Nancy's, and the third paragraph brings you right up against Skinny Nancy's shop window. So each paragraph takes you a stage further into the story.

Once you can recognise how paragraphs work in other people's writing you can use them in your own writing. There are two principles. First you have to decide on the order things should go in and secondly you have to make sure that the things you put together in a paragraph fit together and that you have not included anything irrelevant.

● Practice sorting things out into the right order first. Here is a recipe for cooking boiled rice, the Chinese way. In your groups, unscramble the instructions making sure you get them in the right order.

Ingredients
1 cup long-grained rice
1$\frac{3}{4}$ cups cold water
Preparation
Stir well while rice is still hot so that it will be flaky and each grain will separate.
Place rice in strainer and rinse thoroughly in cold running water. Drain.
Place rice in a 2 quart saucepan.
Bring to boil over a high flame. Turn flame to low, cover and let simmer for 20 minutes until dry.
Add 1$\frac{3}{4}$ cups cold water.

● Compare your version with that of other groups to check that you all agree on the order.

● Now you try it with your own material. In your groups write out the instructions as to how to play a game. It might be a playground game, a board game like monopoly or draughts or a new game you have invented.

You could invent a school rules game rather like snakes and ladders where if you are good you go up the ladder and if you land on a square that represents a broken rule you slide down a snake. If you do work out a game based on school you could include it in the pamphlet for next year's first years which the unit 'Using paragraphs to plan writing' will help you to write.

When you have made up your game and written the instructions or just written out the instructions for a game everyone knows there is only one way to find out if your instructions are any good. Get someone in your group or in another group to play the game strictly according to your instructions.

Was everything in the right order? Remember it's no use saying later, 'I should have told you earlier you have to throw a dice each time you move!'

● Now let's leave instructions and try to write something a little more complicated. Imagine you are going away on holiday and you are

leaving your dog to be looked after by a friend. You are so busy packing that you have not got time to go and tell your friend all about your dog's habits. Write three paragraphs in which you explain all he or she will need to know. The paragraphs could take the following form.

Food and drink
(a) What kind of food? What brand? How much? How often? Is he allowed tit bits? Does he beg?
(b) Does he always need a drink after a meal? Should he have water all the time? Does he drink anything else? Is he used to a drink of tea at breakfast?

Sleeping habits
(a) Where does he normally sleep? Kennel? Basket? Under the bed? On the bed?
(b) Does he dream and bark in his sleep? It might be important to let your friend know that, if he is not to be scared out of his wits in the middle of the night.

Exercise
(a) Night and morning?
(b) Is he to be trusted off the lead?
(c) Does he chase cats, other dogs?

So much for getting things in the right order. Now let's look at avoiding red herrings – red herrings are irrelevant facts. Here is an example. Someone might write about a dog's sleeping habits like this.

Rover likes to sleep under my bed. He'll probably try to get under yours. I suppose it makes him feel more secure. Don't worry if he makes noises in the night. He's only dreaming. He imagines he's chasing cats and his legs move as if he's running and he makes a noise like a stifled bark. Do you dream? I do. I had a horrible dream the other night. I felt I was falling off a cliff. I went down and down until I suddenly woke up with a jolt. Anyway, back to Rover, I hope your mum doesn't mind him sleeping in your room.

The whole section about the dream of falling off a cliff, while it was interesting, was not relevant. It was a red herring. Read through your paragraphs and those of your group and see if you can spot any red herrings.

Unit 27
Looking at paragraphs

Read this story in your groups. Do you see how it is divided into paragraphs? The paragraphs are shown by leaving a line. Remember you can either indent – that is start each new paragraph a little way from the margin – or leave a line between each paragraph.

Buzzing Death

A Of the many vicious pests of Northeastern India, the tree bee, half cousin of the Indian hornet, tops the list. These bees go about in immense swarms, making their hives in the highest trees. Unlike the hornet, which will sting only when thoroughly annoyed, the tree bee has the habit of swooping down in attacking thousands, for no apparent reason, and chasing one for his life.

B One sunny morning, riding along a dusty cart track, I found myself, without the least warning, the centre of such an assault. The sky above me suddenly became thick with bees. With an icy shiver down my spine, I put my pony, Souvenir, to a gallop. Flight seemed the only hope of safety, but Souvenir's speed availed us nothing; the bees were after us in earnest. Souvenir jumped, bucked, reared and lashed out in all directions to rid himself of the bees, while I, attempting to protect my face and limbs, had the greatest difficulty in retaining my saddle. In a few moments, an angry buck while turning a corner at full gallop threw me into the dust.

C With less than a mile to safety, I began to leg it with far greater determination than I had ever done in my life. But I was covered from head to foot with bees; they crawled in thousands all over me stinging with excruciating pain. The under-rim of my topee became an angry hive, bees clustered inches deep. My forehead, ears and neck were blanketed in a buzzing, stinging swab of agony. Bees crawled inside my open-necked shirt and up my unprotecting shorts; they were everywhere. I tore them away in handfuls, but only to make room for others about me in clouds.

D As I staggered on I yelled frantically to distant workers; but seeing the swarms about me, they bolted in every direction but mine. Gasping for breath, each time I opened my swollen mouth, more bees entered, until my tongue was stung to twice its normal size, and I was crunching them with my teeth. My nostrils had swollen into uselessness; my eyes, stung and running with water, were rapidly closing.

E Stumbling weakly into the factory compound, I groped my way toward a building that was being erected. As soon as the men working there saw the droning battle array accompanying me, they made for cover at top speed. With the certainty of being half killed themselves, there was no alternative for them.

F I was now a pitiful specimen, blind and deaf, and only able to breathe with extreme difficulty. Scrambling about with unseeing eyes ended by my falling unexpectedly into a huge heap of something soft and powdery, which I sensed must be a mound of red brick dust, used for building purposes. I quickly found myself in a worse quandary, brick dust choking out what little life I had remaining, and the angry swarm concentrating a renewed attack on my lower regions. Withdrawing from the brick dust, I used my remaining strength in a search for the water tank I knew was near. Staggering about in circles, I tore bees from my face and crushed them in handfuls, until I went down in a state of coma, powerless to defend myself. The bees had won.

G After what seemed a lifetime, an unpleasant sensation of great heat swept over me. Presently I faintly felt the touch of human hands as rescuers hurried me away to safety. The reaction proved too strong, and I passed out.

H My timely rescue was effected by two quick-witted Ghurkas, who had raced to a thatch stack and, bringing bundles of dry grass, had quickly surrounded me with a dense wall of fire and smoke, until the bees were beaten off. Later, as I lay unconscious, while the district was being scoured for a doctor, these same two staunch men insisted upon remaining and extracting stings from my inflamed carcass. It took two days to free my body of the discarded stings. When, eventually, I recovered consciousness I was beamingly informed that I had had at least two thousand punctures, probably a record.

I I lay in torment for several days, unable to move. My body, blown up like an oversized sausage, was black, blue and purple, and as hard as frozen meat. For several days I could see and speak only with the greatest difficulty, and it took many applications of anti-swelling lotions before what had once been my nose and ears again emerged from the general mess.

J My convalescence was a lengthy business of some six months in the hospital and several weeks in the cool hills of Darjeeling. When I returned to my old haunts I could never refrain from ducking and looking for the nearest cover whenever a droning swarm passed overhead.

● Now discuss in your groups what the topic of each paragraph is. Each one is labelled with a

different letter. You should try to write just one sentence which sums up what each paragraph is about. For example:

Paragraph C – The man runs for safety while being stung all over by thousands of bees.

When you have done this for each paragraph, discuss why each one is a separate sense unit. Can you see that the paragraphs help you to follow the action of the story in that each stage has its own section?

Now look at the first and last paragraphs (A and J). They have a rather different function. They are not really part of the action.

The first paragraph *introduces* the whole story. It outlines the habits of the tree bee and their delight in chasing people. The last paragraph *concludes* the story. We know before that point that the man will survive his ordeal, but it brings the story to an end by describing his convalescence and later fear of the tree bee.

These introductory and concluding paragraphs are very useful because one tells us what the passage is going to be about and the other sums up what we have been told. When you are reading something you want to be sure you have understood, it is often very useful to go back to the introductory and concluding paragraphs to check that you have got the gist of the passage. They are often useful too, if you are not sure if the passage is going to cover the topics you want. Rather than reading all the way through you can look at these two paragraphs and see whether the passage or the chapter might be likely to be of use to you.

● Here is a newspaper article about bees. All the paragraphs have been removed. In your groups discuss where they should be. You need not rewrite the whole story, but you should write down the line number and the word with which each paragraph should end.

Facing up to Killer Bees

The man defying these 'killer' bees is Professor Helmuth Wiese of Florianpolis Apiculture Unit in Brazil. He believes that the stories about the killer potential of these African Adsonii bees are exaggerated. The bees, which produce twice as much honey as the more gentle English bee, were introduced to Brazil from Africa in 1956. The 48 imported queens were specially selected to breed with domestic ones. But one year later they escaped, bred in their millions and spread. They are now said to be approaching North America, killing as they go: around 200 people and thousands of animals have died. It is not their sting that is so deadly but their method of attack. They sting up to 60 times a minute in a non-stop onslaught lasting up to two hours. Although one person is said to have survived 2243 stings, 400–500 are usually fatal.

Unit 28
Using paragraphs to plan writing

We have seen that paragraphs are used to indicate that everything in them is about the same topic. Now how do you set about joining up paragraphs to do a longer piece of writing?

● Imagine that you are asked to write a guide to your school for next year's first years. What kind of things would you want to include? What things did you find puzzling at first? What things took you ages to work out? Discuss this in your groups and produce a list. Don't forget the information you have already prepared in earlier units – the school language dictionary, the 'school rules' game, who's who in the school, what different languages and dialects there might be in a class like yours.

Your list might look something like this:

number of lessons in the day
what happens if you are late
when the library is open
the dinner routine
parents' evenings
what books you can borrow from the library
when school starts and finishes
what sports kit you need
how often you get homework
what a form tutor is
why you need a sturdy bag
what happens at break-time
what a year head is
map of the school
what new subjects you are taught
when you need absence notes
how you get to school
how many languages and dialects are spoken in a class like yours
your 'school rules' game
what uniform, if any, you need
what clubs you can join

who's who in the school
what sports activities are available
when you get reports
a dictionary of school language

At this stage your ideas are in no particular order. You could probably write a paragraph about each item but the finished piece of writing would not be very useful, because you would be jumping from topic to topic.

● Look again at your list and try to link topics which seem to go together. Your new list might look like this:

number of lessons in the day
when school starts and finishes
what happens at breaktime
the dinner routine

when the library is open
what books you can borrow

what a form tutor is
what a year head is
who's who in the school

how often you get homework
why you need a sturdy bag

your 'school rules' game

a dictionary of school language
some languages and dialects spoken in school

what sports kit you need
what uniform, if any, you need

when you get reports
parents' evenings

when you need absence notes
what happens when you are late

what sports activities are available
what new subjects are taught
what clubs you can join

map of the school
how you get to school

Having put together those topics that seem related, you next have to decide on an order. How do you do this? It all depends on the emphasis you want. If you want to convince next year's first year that they are coming to an exciting new school you might start with descriptions of all the new subjects that are going to be taught, the games they can play and the clubs they can join. If you think that the most important thing to sort out first is the daily routine, then you will start with that. Some groups of topics link up with other groups, and so should go with them. When you are discussing the daily routine, you will also need to discuss what a form tutor and a year head do and also who's who in the school. This would also be the time to talk about what happens if you are late and when you need to bring notes to school.

The only thing that is not fitted in is the map of the school and how to get to it. This will need to be drawn up by you and if it is properly drawn and labelled it will not need any explanation. You should decide whether to include this at the beginning or the end of your piece of writing, but it will probably not be needed in the middle. You may need to refer to it. If you have to report to an office if you arrive late in the morning, then you will need to explain this in your section on what happens if you are late; you will need to say something like, 'When you arrive late you must go to the general office. This is labelled for you on the attached map.'

You might also decide to draw a diagram of who's who in your school. This is explained in the unit on 'The language of school' (see page 60). It is simpler to draw a diagram like this than to make a long, dull list.

● In your groups now re-order your list of topics so that the final order makes sense and your ideas are no longer in a jumble. The next thing to do is to divide up the topics so that everyone in the group does some of the writing.

Before you start to write you should think carefully about who you are writing for – your audience. Try to write for someone like yourself – your age. You will need to write simply but don't 'talk down' to your reader. Imagine you are writing to a friend. If you know someone at your old primary school who might be coming to your new school write as if you were talking to him or her.

When this has been done, read through each other's work. You can correct spelling and punctuation errors that others may have missed. You can use the proof-reading signs we looked at in the unit on proof-reading.

Most important, check that all the vital information has been covered. Ask yourself two questions:

1 Does this tell me everything I wanted to know last September?
2 If it was my first day at this school, would I understand this?

When each group has finished you will have produced an interesting pamphlet on your school. The class can edit a final version and have copies made for next year's first years.

Unit 29
Using diagrams to plan writing

Now you understand the process of planning, making lists, ordering and re-ordering, you can try using a diagram to plan your writing rather than writing and rewriting lists.

For the guide to your school you might have started like this:

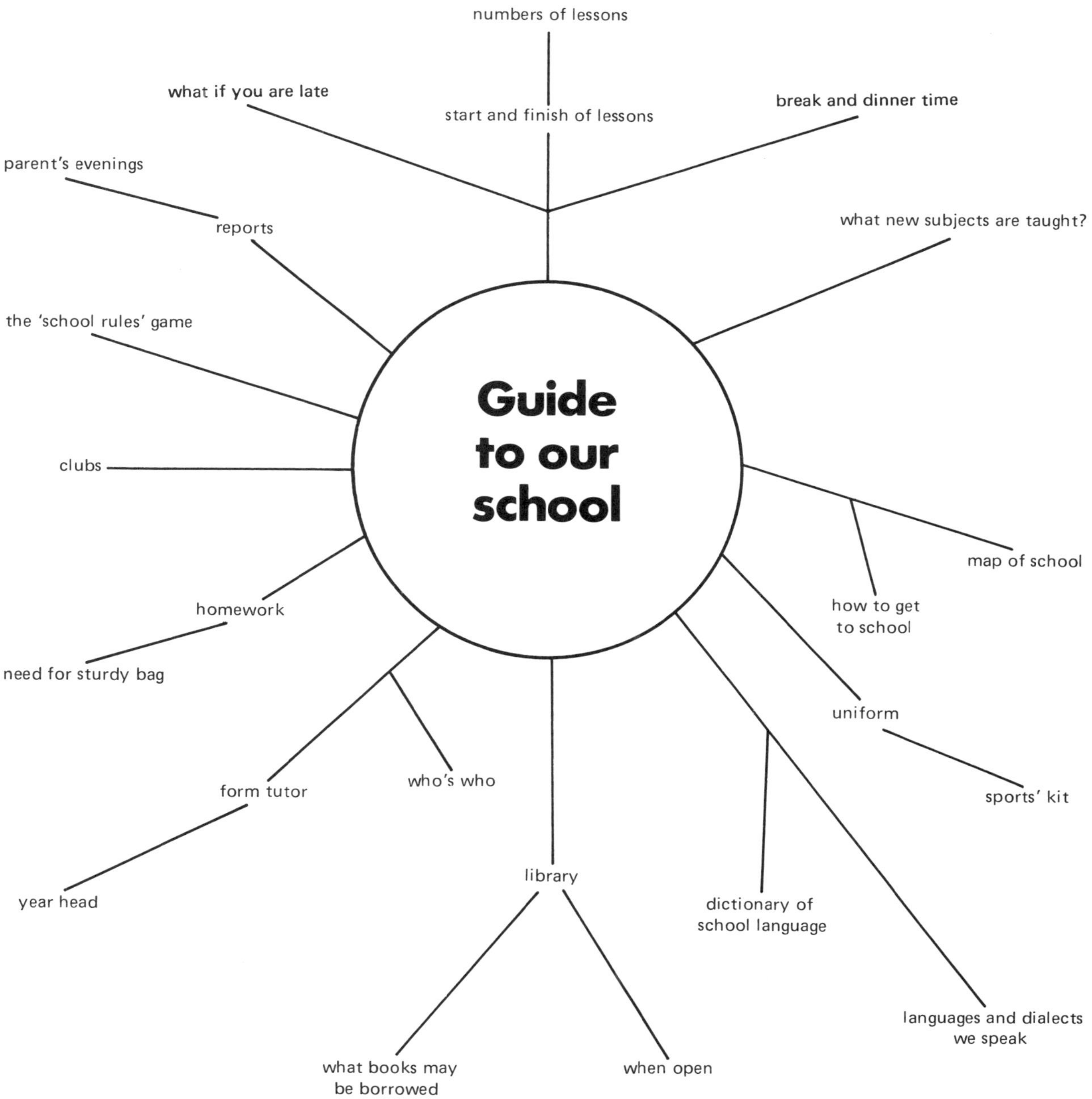

numbers of lessons

what if you are late

start and finish of lessons

break and dinner time

parent's evenings

reports

what new subjects are taught?

the 'school rules' game

Guide to our school

clubs

map of school

how to get to school

homework

need for sturdy bag

uniform

form tutor

who's who

sports' kit

year head

library

dictionary of school language

what books may be borrowed

when open

languages and dialects we speak

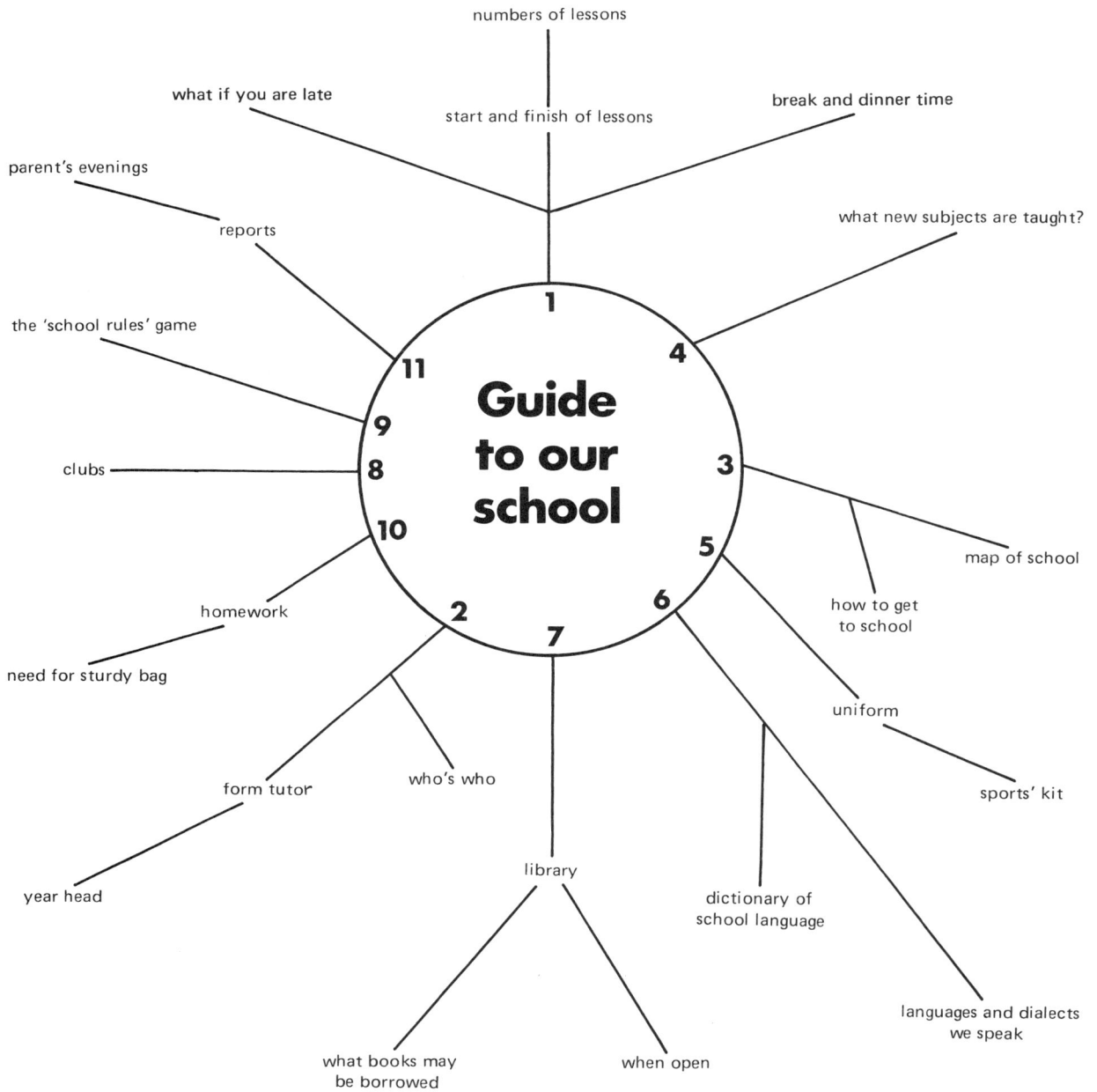

numbers of lessons

what if you are late

start and finish of lessons

break and dinner time

parent's evenings

reports

what new subjects are taught?

the 'school rules' game

1

4

11

Guide to our school

9

clubs

8

3

10

5

map of school

homework

2

7

6

how to get to school

need for sturdy bag

form tutor

who's who

uniform

year head

sports' kit

library

dictionary of school language

what books may be borrowed

when open

languages and dialects we speak

You take the central topic and follow ideas which develop from it. As you think of new ideas you merely add them to the line they seem most suited to.

This diagram gives you as much information as your second list. All you have to do is decide which big topics should go with which other big topics to enable you to sort out your final order. You can do this final order by adding numbers to the diagram. If you decide to start with the daily routine add a large 1 to the diagram where the daily routine section meets the circle. If you are going on to form tutor, year heads and who's who in the school then write a large 2 inside the circle where that line meets it. You continue this process until you have got everything in order like on page 94.

● Now you try using diagrams to plan writing. In your groups plan a little pamphlet about how to use your school library. Draw your circle with the lines leading off it for all the topics you need to discuss. Then work out the order in which you are going to write about them and number the lines as a reminder. Then write up the pamphlet using the diagram as a guide to the order of the paragraphs.

Again you will have to think carefully about who you are preparing the pamphlet for – other pupils in your school? next year's first years? visitors to the school?

Then you should proof-read and edit your writing as before.

Glossary

This is a list of the technical terms used in this book and their meanings.

The meanings given to the words are the meanings they have in *context*. For example, there are many meanings of the word *stress*, but the one given here is the meaning that *stress* has in the passage in which it appears.

accent – a particular way of pronouncing words

adjectives – words which describe nouns, e.g. *red* dress

adverb – a word which describes a *verb* e.g. Susan walked *slowly* or an *adjective* e.g. the *really* large book

body language – the use of gestures or facial expressions to communicate. This may or may not be accompanied by words.

cloze – a passage from which words have been missed out. The students' task is to use context clues to guess which words are missing.

context clues – clues we get about the meaning of words from the sentence, or passage in which they appear

dialect – a version of a language which has its own special words and its own grammar

dialogue – a conversation between two or more people in a story or play

fillers – a word like 'um', 'er', 'you know' which we use in conversation. They are part of the rhythm of speech. We don't use them in writing unless we are writing dialogue.

gesture – a movement of part of the body to express an idea or emotion

guide words – the words which appear at the top of the page in a dictionary, and help you find words quickly

ideograph – a picture which represents an idea

nouns – words which can fit a gap like:
I saw the . . . . yesterday.
The names of people or places are also nouns.

proof-reading – re-reading your work to look for errors

punctuation – symbols which we use when we transfer speaking to writing

quotation marks – symbols which show that someone is speaking e.g. She said, 'I am angry'.

received pronounciation – an accent which gives no clues about where a speaker has lived

scanning – glancing through a passage or a map or picture to find a particular piece of information.

skimming – glancing at a passage to pick out the general idea

standard English – a dialect of English which is understood by all speakers and readers of English

stress – the emphasis we place on syllables within words, e.g. audacious (aw-day-shus)

syllable – a unit of sound e.g. table has two syllables: tab – le

transcript – an exact written version of speech

verbs – words which can change their tense e.g. love, loved

vocabulary – a range of words that you find in a language or in a dialect of a language